BILL THE GOAT'S ADULT REFRESHER GUIDE TO WRITING

Bruce Fleming

University Press of America,® Inc.
Lanham · Boulder · New York · Toronto · Plymouth, UK

Copyright © 2008 by
Bruce Fleming

University Press of America,® Inc.
4501 Forbes Boulevard
Suite 200
Lanham, Maryland 20706
UPA Acquisitions Department (301) 459-3366

Estover Road
Plymouth PL6 7PY
United Kingdom

All rights reserved
Printed in the United States of America
British Library Cataloging in Publication Information Available

Library of Congress Control Number: 2007933319
ISBN-13: 978-0-7618-3892-0 (paperback : alk. paper)
ISBN-10: 0-7618-3892-9 (paperback : alk. paper)

∞™ The paper used in this publication meets the minimum
requirements of American National Standard for Information
Sciences—Permanence of Paper for Printed Library Materials,
ANSI Z39.48—1984

Preface · *v*

I
Begin Here · *1*

1. Three categories · 2. Write for Bill · 3. Problems · 4. Purpose · 5. Adulthood · 6. Think structurally · 7. Respect · 8. Tool kit · 9. Bill isn't you · 10. You are in charge · 11. Get some sleep · 12. Being normal · 13. Pay attention · 14. An alternative · 15. Speed limits · 16. The magic trick · 17. Spectrum of possibilities · 18. The dreaded five-paragraph essay · 19. On beyond simple · 20. Stepping off the path · 21. Bending rules · 22. Moo · 23. Photographs · 24. 4'2" · 25. Because he was Faulkner · 26. E.I.

II
Follow These Principles · *19*

1. Don't block the tube · 2. Prepare for Inspection · 3. Be like Michelangelo · 4. Fill the hole · 5. Make sure it's the right size · 6. Deal with the monster in your room · 7. Know what your most important point is · 8. Don't be coy · 9. Don't frustrate Bill · 10. Make your course clear in advance · 11. Say it once · 12. Get the level of importance right · 13. Know the difference between writing time and your time · 14. Anticipate reactions · 15. Don't mountain-top · 16. Know what the deal-breakers are · 17. Understand the medium · 18. Ask, How's it going to look in print? · 19. Don't think like a midshipman · 20. Be clear in your reference · 21. Avoid clichés · 22. Don't ballpark · 23. Don't make statements that won't pass muster · 24. Stage public executions · 25. Showcase your best muscles · 26. Don't overdrive your headlights · 27. Feed Baby Bill · 28. Don't get too attached to your own words · 29. Revise · 30. Revise again · 31. Run a perimeter

Table of Contents

III
Your Own Private Grammar Friday

A: Why Study Grammar? • *47*

1. Grammar is scary • 2. What is grammar? • 3. Prescriptive and descriptive grammar • 4. In the pool • 5. To willfully split

B: Bill's Brand of Grammar • *54*

1. The topic • 2. Setting things up • 3. Topic sentences and openers • 4. Maintaining a consistent speed • 5. Paragraphs • 6. Sentences • Long and short sentences • Compound predicates or sentences • 7. Completing patterns • 8. Punctuation • Clusters • Commas • Commas in lists • Coordinate and non-coordinate adjectives • Restrictive and non-restrictive appositives and clauses • "That" and "which" • Comma splices • Semi-colons • Colons • Hyphens • 9. Conjunctions • 10. Word order • Reference • Superman • 11. Awk • Parallelism • 12. Verb tenses • Tense switches • Indirect discourse • 13. "If" clauses • Double conditional • 14. Mistakes are made • 15. Word usage • Langue/parole • Foregrounding meaning • Metaphors • Iced drink • D problems • 16. Nobody's perfect

IV
Correcting Your Own Course • *103*

1. Student papers • 2. Newspaper article

V
How to Read • *123*

1. Strawberry preserves • 2. New ways of seeing • 3. Gizmos • 4. Two kinds of not understanding • 5. Guidance • 6. Notice things • 7. The blind man • 8. Touch • 9. Mickey's three fingers • 10. The Martians came • 11. Descartes' razor • 12. Forks • 13. Reading Shakespeare

Index • *143*

About the Author • *145*

Preface

The world is full of adults who feel apologetic about their writing. They're usually quite competent at what they do for their primary job, which might be being a student. But somehow writing stops them cold: "What do I do now?" they ask, hating once again the blank sheet of paper or computer screen. Others plunge in, knowing they're just spinning their wheels. These are the writers who need *Bill the Goat's Adult Refresher Guide to Writing*.

When you're a student, you can ask the professor. But classes tend to piece together small things into a larger whole: *Bill the Goat's Guide* starts big and explains the small as parts of the whole. You need to hear things from a couple of perspectives to have them make sense anyway. This book is the perfect complement to a writing course. And at some point the class is over.

What do you do when you're not even a student anymore? Once you're grown up, it's a bit embarrassing to admit that you're a bad writer—unless, like some people (largely men, I'd guess, being a man myself), you try to make this weakness into a badge of honor: you think don't have to do it well because you can pay somebody to do it for you. That sounds like the way ladies in pre-modern China were proud of their tiny deformed feet that meant they never had to walk, having servants to lean on. It's better to walk by yourself. But once their student days are over, people tend simply to do the best they can with their writing insufficiencies, relying on friends, subordinates, subsequent correctors with the "writing gift," and the computer to patch up their mistakes. Companies will sometimes organize writing seminars to help wobbly writers, *Bill the Goat's Guide* could help there too.

That means a lot of bad writing is committed daily in offices of all kinds. Usually it's not of a level serious enough to shut down the company or the government. (A computer glitch can do both, however, sometimes the result of bad writing in computer languages.) What all this bad writing does instead is slow things down, causing incomprehension, back-tracking, the necessity to send written work back down the chain of command, and heartburn on the part of the people who have to read it. Inefficiency doesn't always stop the machines, but it always makes them run slower: bad writing costs us all an incalculable amount, in money, in time, and in terms of people's dispositions.

Unlike what I call "What do I do?" grammar books—or even their sophisticated spin-offs, like Strunk and White's now-classic *Elements of Style, Bill the Goat's Adult Refresher Guide to Writing* insists that people can answer all by themselves the question, "What do I do?." But doing so means being clear to themselves about what their goal is. They have to ask themselves, "What's my point?" "What am I trying to get across?" The answers to these questions will almost automatically provide answers to questions like these: "Do I need this distinction or that one?" "Do these elements go together or do they need to be split apart?" "Do I need past or past perfect tense here?" "Is it 'its' or 'it's'?" Taken all together, these equal one question: does Bill the Goat understand it?

Bill the Goat is the mascot of the U.S. Naval Academy, where I've taught writing and literature for more than two decades. Bill is the consumer (he reads, then chews) of everything my students write. I tell them, "Write for Bill!" You can write for Bill too. If you ask: "Does Bill get this?" and make sure he does, your writing worries are over.

However, this is not a quick-fix, visualize-and-you've-got-it book. Merely visualizing Bill won't do anything. There he is, hairy, smelly, but eager to get your point. Now what?

Writing for Bill isn't just a matter of visualizing Bill, but of processing everything you write (sometimes as you write it) as if Bill were reading it—every word, every sentence, every paragraph, every page. You have to see your own work not from your own perspective, but from Bill's.

Seeing it from Bill's perspective, you can tell what he doesn't understand, and why. And that means, you can both identify the problem and try to fix it. If you know what a machine is for and thus understand how it would look it if were functional, you can probably identify a problem by finding the thing that's out of place or broken. Usually you can fix it; sometimes you can't, but at least you know what the problem is and can tell the mechanic. Writing works the same way. Much of writing is the constant process of correcting your own course, sometimes before you get off course: use the right word, a clear construction, a point that follows the one you've just made. It's not true you'll never be stumped, but you can fix most things, and have an idea about what the problem is with others.

Writing for Bill allows you to see your writing the way others do. That's the essence of learning acting too, to name a comparable technical skill: knowing how your actions, grimaces, and intonations will play on the screen, or to the back balcony. Acting is about learning techniques to achieve certain goals, solve certain problems. But if you just learn the techniques in isolation from each other, you'll be lost when you're faced with a real text you have to learn. You're not a good actor or writer unless you have the sense of having access to a vast repertory of tools and techniques you can draw on depending on the circumstances, and unless you understand these circumstances when you see them. Language is slippery; there's no list of how-tos that will solve all problems. A Chinese proverb notes that it's better to be taught to fish for yourself than to be given fish. Bill gives a few fish, just to be friendly, but he's mainly concerned with teaching how to fish.

All writing has to be writing for your particular Bill, whoever he is (defining your Bill is one of the first steps in writing). Some guides to writing express a related idea by saying, Remember your audience. But usually they mean only, use the right tone (not too casual for a formal audience, not too formal for a casual one), remember to explain things your audience doesn't know, and give people what they want to hear (if you want them to buy what you've written). All these are important, but writing for Bill goes beyond this. It also means remembering, among other things, that Bill ingests your words not in the order you think of them but in the order they appear on the page. Bill is condemned to eat your writing like a string of spaghetti: the beginning comes before the middle and both of these come before the end. Bill can't edit the string of spaghetti, re-arrange it so it's closer to what's in your head. Bill has no access to your head, only to the spaghetti on the page. Successful writing is making something that works as spaghetti, whatever went on in your head beforehand.

Bill the Goat's Adult Refresher Guide to Writing takes a holistic approach to writing: the various ways you can achieve your purpose (whatever that is) aren't in separate mental files; they're all jumbled together. Sometimes your option if you don't want to or can't do X is not Y, but instead B—or you could re-conceive the whole thing and do P and Q instead. And getting something right doesn't matter if a more important something is wrong: everything has to click at the same time. You can get all the commas right, but have a non-starter of a topic. The order of your ideas may be so out of whack that Bill can't even appreciate your fancy word choices. Everything fits together.

That's the way it is in life too. When you go out on a date, you have to look nice, smell nice, dress well, have interesting things to say, have clean teeth and shirt, arrive on time, and not talk about your ex. So many things! If you do too much on one, you may neglect the others. So instead of adding up the parts, you have to conceive of the whole effect you're hoping to have and work backwards from that. If you don't see yourself the way your date does, you don't stand a chance of getting enough of the specifics right at once to pass muster, or have a second date.

Bill the Goat's Adult Refresher Guide to Writing helps you fix your writing while you continue to write. After all, you're an adult, whether a young or an old one. Reading this book is like going to the golf pro to improve your game. Probably you won't kill anybody if you continue to play the way you do. But you'll get better at the game if you understand why Bill is always looking so grumpy, and you'll feel better about yourself. The world will look rosier, and Bill will be much happier too.

This, finally, is a book to be read, rather than a reference book—though parts of it can serve as reference too (I'm thinking of the section on "Grammar Fridays"). It has a beginning, middle and end; it's not just a series of isolated observations. It starts big, gets precise, and then branches out. In its own way, it has a sort of plot. Read it at home, in bed, on the beach. It's meant to be fun.

What it isn't is school-marmy. Far too many people associate writing with sharp-nosed Miss Smith in the 9th grade who screeched and wore funny cologne. Bill doesn't wear any cologne at all, and he certainly doesn't screech. Besides, he's your buddy. Everybody's grown up now; this is about you taking responsibility for getting through to Bill and getting better at what you do—not about being right or wrong. In real life, as opposed to school, we're rarely all right or all wrong, just more or less effective. *Bill the Goat's Adult Refresher Guide to Writing* is about making you more effective in your writing, whoever your particular Bill might be.

July 2007
Annapolis, Maryland

I
Start Here

1. Three categories

There are three categories of people who need *Bill the Goat's Adult Refresher Guide to Writing*. The first category is people who get cold chills of fear when they have to write something. They sit in front of a blank piece of paper or computer screen wondering where to begin and how to proceed. Or they stop midway in a personal letter wondering what to write next. They need Bill to help them get over their fear.

The second category of people who need this book is those people who have no fear and should. Usually these are people whose idea of writing is e-mails and Instant Messsages on the computer. These people have forgotten that this sort of writing isn't the only kind of writing. They write official reports in the same way they write an Instant Message and wonder why their boss is unhappy. Remembering Bill will help the too-fearless ones be aware of the many circumstances that people write under so they can produce what's needed for a specific set of circumstances.

The third category, probably the largest, is all the people in the middle. They want to do it right and do have some idea about how to get started, but sometimes are stopped dead by things they're unsure about. How should I structure my writing? Is it "who" or "whom"? Do I do it this way or do I do it that way?

This third category includes many functioning adults, ranging from students who can barely vote to CEOs of major organizations. Most of the time we do things we know how to do. Sometimes we grind to a halt. Sometimes we think we know what to do, but aren't quite sure we're right. We find ourselves in a gray area.

2. Write for Bill

Bill the Goat is the mascot of the U.S. Naval Academy, where I've taught literature and writing for more than two decades. A midshipman in a Bill suit comes to most varsity games, and a real goat named Bill (by now Bill XXIII or so, I think) kept for that purpose is led out on the football field. Some of the midshipmen are Bill wranglers (handlers). That's their job at football games.

Bill can be your mascot too. The most fundamental thing a midshipman, or any writer, can learn is this: all writing is for Bill. I tell midshipmen to buy themselves a stuffed Bill the Goat in the Naval Academy store and sit him on the chair in front of them. Write the paper glancing frequently at Bill. When you read it over silently, ask: does Bill get it? Then read it out loud to Bill.

Your Bill need not, in fact, be a stuffed goat—or even a real one. It can be a book, a desk toy, or an imaginary friend. But I've found Bill works best.

3. Problems

Bad writing slows down the machinery of business, academics, and the military. It causes countless problems, financial and otherwise. Usually it doesn't bring the machines to a complete halt, it just slows them down and makes them far more inefficient than they have to be. But we don't have to wait for the machinery to grind to a complete stop before doing something about it; just because the patient isn't dead doesn't mean we don't need doctors. And sometimes, as a result of not being treated, the patient does die. If we don't do something about the sand in the machines, they do eventually stop.

Good writing, writing for Bill, keeps things nicely oiled and humming along. You can make things fast with machines that work well.

4. Purpose

Writing for Bill helps people think about the purpose of what they're doing rather than merely following rules. Understanding the purpose of your actions rather than following a list of how-tos is the key to reaching adulthood in life, and it's the key to becoming a writer-adult too. Many people who are functioning adults in other ways are still not writer-adults, because they have never been taught to think of the purpose of what they're doing.

The end result we're aiming at as we clear the table after a meal is that the dishes are in the dishwasher and the table is clean and ready for the next meal. Small children don't know this. So you have to give them a list of steps to follow. Such as: take the napkins off the table. Pick up the spoon, please. When they get older they can visualize the cleared table, so you say merely: Could you clear the table please? When they get yet older they realize that the room has to be ready to go again, and clearing the table itself becomes part of an even larger whole, the daily rhythm.

Most writers, through no fault of their own, are still at the level of "Pick up the spoon." Each step has to be spelled out. This is so because they're not thinking of what they're aiming at. If they get to the point where they can think of end result, which is to say think of Bill, of course they'll still have to pick up the spoon. But they won't think of this as a discrete act or an end in itself, any more than someone who is driving to work thinks of putting the car in gear as an end in itself. Thinking of what you want the writing to look like when you're done—understanding the purpose, thinking of Bill—allows you to answer your questions based on the extent to which your options achieve the goal.

This means that many individual questions unify into the larger purpose. You answer the questions as you go along; you're not left at the level of "what do I do next?" or even of "pick up the napkins" or "turn the key."

5. Adulthood

People achieve adulthood in writing, as they do in other things as well, when they come to understand what the purpose might be of all those things they've learned to do "just because."

Normally I put aprons on my two little boys in their high chairs. One day, all aprons are in the wash. Knowing that the purpose of the apron is to keep the food off their clothes, I use towels instead, tying them around two little necks. My three-year-old, however, sees only the object. The towel, it turns out, is completely unacceptable; he wants his apron. We have a discussion. I say: "The towel is okay. Next time, we have aprons again." Finally he agrees, and I've doubled his options.

Seeing in terms of purpose rather than being tied to specific objects is the basis of what nowadays is called "thinking outside the box." It's also the basis of the inventiveness of disaster movies, which typically pit one man against people trying to blow up Fill-in-the-blank (a building, the Western World). The hero is always shown putting daily objects to unheard-of uses: a fork becomes a detonating device, a rope is something to save yourself from disaster; a scouring pad is part of an ingenious microwave bomb. If you're tied to the world, or to the typical purpose of objects, you can't use things in new ways.

6. Think structurally

So part of understanding what you're doing with writing is understanding language structurally, in terms of point rather than the words in front of you. If you're stuck at the level of thinking that only a bib, or perhaps even more specifically your favorite blue bib, is an acceptable object to keep food off your shirt, you will stop dead realizing the bib is out of the running: What do I do without my bib? Is it "it's" or "its"? You have no way to answer. Structural thinking is understanding what that little squiggle we call an apostrophe is doing there: it makes a contraction of two words. "It's" = it is. "Its" is the same series as "his" and "hers." Which do you want here? You're suddenly able to answer, because you know what information you want to convey. Even if you don't know, you've narrowed the question down and can look it up. Suddenly you know how to solve the problem; you're not helpless.

7. Respect

There's no convincing evidence that people have gotten dumber in the last century. But there is evidence that good writing is threatened. I think this is because categories one and three above are growing: people are either too fearful or writing, or not fearful enough. We shouldn't fear writing, but we do need to respect it. People who whip off the first thing that comes to them, in the way that it comes to them, are probably not showing enough respect for writing. Which means, not enough respect for Bill.

8. Tool kit

Most people can achieve solid writing, in the same way that most of us can respond to the normal demands of our household living with the tool kit containing hammer, nails, screwdriver, and drill.

Before I left for vacation one year during the period I lived in Africa, I handed my cook/gardener/fixit man a Swiss army knife. When I got back, I had a fence and a banana-leaf-thatched gazebo in my backyard.

With his ingenuity and muscles and the portable tool kit in a pocket-knife, he'd made me a whole little world. He visualized the result, so every sawed pole and woven banana leaf was, rather than an end in itself, a means to the end. When he asked himself, Do I do it this way or that way? he was able to answer the question, because he knew what the result was supposed to be. He even knew when the two options he had were equally good, so he could just pick one: he wasn't frozen between two alternatives. This book is the tool kit, the Swiss army knife. You have to define what you're going to do with it.

9. Bill isn't you

Bill is sitting on the chair in front of you. He's not inside your head. He's outside. You have to get the ideas out of your head, through the strange transmission medium of scratches on the page, and over to Bill. You had to learn that turning a wheel in front of you made the car under you go in this direction or that. In the same way, you have to learn that making these scratches cause this or that reaction in Bill. Just as ideas have to be translated into clicks to work in Morse code, so they have to be translated into symbols on the page to be transmissible as writing.

10. You are in charge

A number of years ago I had a student who had turned down an athletic scholarship to an Ivy League university in favor of attending the Naval Academy because he "wanted a challenge." He was bright and exuded limitless energy. He was, however, a less than stellar writer, something I as his senior thesis advisor felt very keenly. He graduated and returned to the Academy to teach our plebes after five years of flying airplanes. I realized that somehow, he'd turned a corner in those five years. Now he wrote well: he got his points across, he didn't make mistakes, he stayed on message.

"So tell me," I said to him one day, "what happened?"

He grinned. "I finally got some responsibility," he said. He had suddenly realized that he was in charge of getting through to Bill. He couldn't rely on anyone else. "That," he added, "and I got some sleep."

11. Get some sleep

Far too many people think that you can go into a writing session tired. They think that because you're sitting in a chair when you write rather than lifting weights or pushing a lawnmower, you're not doing anything that requires energy. They're wrong.

Writing is one of the most intense experiences there is: you're constantly "on," turning what comes out of you into something that will process as it goes into Bill. It's a continual exercise of seeing things the way Bill does, rather than as you do. The experience is like playing a fast video game: things are coming at you right and left, you alone can save the world. Will you survive? You change sentences around, move things up or down, clarify ideas, resolve inconsistencies, substitute one word for another, and re-configure paragraphs when you realize you've ended up in a different place than you thought you would. If you're sleep-deprived you move sluggishly, you fail to see things that later appear obvious, you can't organize your ideas, and you use the wrong word where you should have used the right one.

We exist, during the process of writing, only to move marks around. All viewers see is our fingers going up and down on the keys, or pushing a pen. What they don't see is the fireworks going off inside our heads, a thousand decisions a minute. It's all about those marks, the way a chess game is about moving little figures around on a board. Get some sleep.

12. Being normal

Writing means using a very complex tool box of tools to produce reactions in Bill. Though the tools are numerous, they aren't infinite in number. They're what you're given to work with: you have to use a "?" to indicate a question, because that's what Bill understands. You can invent new tools if they're visibly related to the old, but you can't switch the tools around with no reason, and you can't do anything you like.

At least this is true if you're a normal person with a professional life. Having a professional life for most of us means, we write for people who will not forgive us just because we're us. We don't matter as individuals to other people we write for, we matter only as writers. To our families, by contrast, virtually all of us matter as individuals. So you can probably get away with not writing well to your parents or spouse.

A small group of people exist in something of the same relationship with respect to the world as we all do to our parents. If you're a politician or a movie star, your physical presence and the prestige of what you do makes up the difference between correct expression and Bill's ear, just as the fact that you're your parents' child means they're probably going to be thrilled by anything you do. This is true also for anyone who has subordinates whose job is to make them look good in public. If you're a star, a politician, or a CEO, the cracks will be filled in, the context supplied, and *voilà*: you will, it seems, have said or written something cogent and useful.

It's not a good idea even for people in high places to accept this kind of adulation; the rest of us will never be offered it. If politicians or business executives think the reason anything they write is greeted with smiles is that it's actually clear and logical, rather than that they are who they are, they'll be surprised the day they retire, lose an election, or get another job. It's always better to get real respect for real accomplishments than to get pretend respect for non-existent accomplishments. Real respect from people means real desire to do what you ask, rather than pretend. And that in turn means you have some chance of getting the thing done.

In the short run, people surrounded by subordinates whose job is to explain away their mistakes with "clarifications" admittedly do not need *Bill the Goat's Adult Refresher Guide to Writing*. The rest of us do.

13. Pay attention

You don't need a professor to tell you how language is used if you pay attention. How do you think the professor came to know how language is used? Everyone is born into language. It's been going on long before we arrived on the scene, and it will be going on for a long while after we're gone. We don't create language, except to the extent that we do. We humans are like pipe organs: we're nothing but channels for the air that whooshes through us, the flow of language that has been around forever and will be around forever. But we're the ones who channel it into specific sounds.

All of us can learn by listening and reading what combinations are used for what things. What do we do to show that one idea is most important? How do we express doubt? How do we show disdain? Do we say "cowed from" something? (No: "cowed by.") "Make up with" is not the same as "make up to." The way we make clear to Bill that two contrasting points of view on an unresolved issue are coming his way is by saying "on the one hand... on the other" (not: "on the one hand, but finally").

People find themselves without the tools to write because they haven't paid attention when the tools were being handed out. And that's all the time. So: pay attention when you read things written with an eye to Bill (such as any national newspaper), or when people used to speaking speak. You have to be paying attention all the time because we learn these things randomly, in no particular order. Grammar books and courses arrange them in logical order. This kind of artificial classroom arrangement gives us the illusion that we learn things in an organized fashion. By paying attention to one short piece of writing, you can learn how a certain word is used, a new way to use the colon, and a turn of phrase you never knew existed. Too many people think that language is something an authority figure will impart to them a few times a week at specific times. It's the assumption that the language isn't theirs that makes them deaf to it. They think: it's not my responsibility.

But it is. And language isn't something that happens three times a week in English class. It's going on around you all the time.

14. An alternative

Bill the Goat's Adult Refresher Guide provides an alternative to the now-classic Strunk and White *Elements of Style*. Strunk and White tell you what to do. To some degree, they tell you why. What they don't tell you is how to think it out for yourself.

If Strunk and White were writing a guide to good driving, they'd tell you: "Use your turn signal." If people actually took such rules to heart and used their turn signals, we might argue it doesn't matter that they are merely acting mechanically, without understanding the reason. But people tend not to use their turn signals, even though they know they should. This is so because most people resent rules they don't understand. "Use your turn signal" is something that will be perceived as a limitation on freedom. Cheating on it is only natural, if you can get away with it.

15. Speed limits

If the speed limit is thought just a limit but as a limitation, there will be no reason not to exceed it if you can get away with it. Many people get adolescent joy out of doing so.

Bill would say: "Speed limits have been set up by people who have actually driven the roads to see what's safe, or as a result of a general law (say, 25 mph. along residential roads) that has a purpose: kids dart out suddenly."

Does this mean you'd never be justified in speeding? No, but each exception needs to be justified. You'd be mowed down if you went the speed limit on the New Jersey Turnpike. Or: your wife is having a baby, and you can see the road is absolutely clear. At least you don't perceive the limit as merely a foreign imposition that it's your duty to resist.

I spend my life with intelligent young adults whose writing education has consisted largely of rules like "Use your turn signal." Many of them don't, and many of them resent having to do so. The hours I spend with them are intended to get them to see the reasons for the rules. "Oh," they say. "I never thought of that."

16. The magic trick

By posing the question clearly the question disappears: you see how to solve it. That's the magic trick I'm trying to teach in *Bill the Goat's Adult Refresher Guide*. Ask: what do I need to tell Bill? If you can say what this is, you can probably do it, or at least figure out how.

17. Spectrum of possibilities

Strunk and White's rules work best for simple situations. They recommend writing that is simple, clear, and direct. But this is only one end of a long spectrum, one alternative among many. What about the rest?

If we're writing a personal letter, we typically structure with some reference to the last letter, to establish continuity, and then to a chronological version of intervening affairs before arriving at a fuller version of events closer in time. And a novel has entirely different rules. In reading a novel, we store up a good deal of information before we demand to see the pattern; we establish the pattern in a different way than we ask for the point in a memorandum. If we judge novels by Struck and White's criteria for writing we'll be puzzled.

An example of writing at Strunk and White's end of the spectrum are the memoranda which are sent out by the Naval Academy administration to the student body, the Brigade of Midshipmen.

All military memoranda are very clear about who they're from. In fact, they're so clear the first line is "From." They're equally clear about who they're to: the next line is "To." They're clear about their subject, which has to be easily summarizable. After all, the next line says "Subject."

Then follows the body of the memo. Its audience comes from the same small, enclosed world as the sender, in our case the Naval Academy. This means everybody who reads it knows the same basic facts about this world. Common information is usually summarized under the rubric "Background." As in: "Recently we have been experiencing problems with the air conditioning system in Bancroft Hall." Then comes "Problem," which is the particular impetus for the memo, the thing that everybody doesn't know. (If they did, there would be no memo, or it would be part of "Background" rather than "Problem.") For example: "Yesterday, 11 April, the air conditioning ceased operating completely. It turned out this was due to X" and so on. What to do? This is addressed next, under the rubric of "Action."

This is clear. But this memo is to the rest of writing as a military parade is to sidewalk traffic on Fifth Avenue. New Yorkers are never going to move in step, and the rest of the world is never going to be as rigid as this memo. Nor would we want it to be. If you don't understand how all these kinds of writing fit together you can't decide which is appropriate, and how to do the other kinds, the ones that aren't like memos.

18. The dreaded five-paragraph essay

Students frequently come to me having learned a form of writing I call "the dreaded five-paragraph essay," which is almost a parody of the Strunk and White end of the spectrum. The first paragraph opens like this: "In this paper, I intend to cover three topics: A, B, and C." Each of the subsequent three paragraphs covers one of these, in the order listed (when the essay is correctly written). The last paragraph announces: "In this paper I have covered three topics, A, B, and C."

The problem with this template is not that it's ineffective, any more than saying "Did you have a good week-end?" to a colleague every Monday morning is ever inappropriate. That's the formulaic question. You can say it every Monday, and every Monday it will be appropriate, unless you know someone close to the colleague died that weekend.

But of course it's predictable, and after a time you are all too conscious of the fact that the relationship has not matured beyond the same formulaic back and forth. Sometimes that's just what you need. If such a greeting is exchanged with a far-off superior, then it's likely to stay just this conventional. If it's part of a conversation with an equal, however, we may try and warm things up a bit, ask something different for once, or get more personal.

The conventional social question, like the five-paragraph essay, or the military memo listing "Background," and "Problem," all have their place. High school students learn the five-paragraph essay the way they learn "Put on your turn signal." They've learned to drill on the parade field, the rigid completely formulaic motions of the march-on and the gun handling called the Manual of Arms. But they don't know anything else. What do they do on the dance floor?

19. On beyond simple

Some day you may be required to do something completely different than write a memo. You might have to inspire the troops, which requires some eloquence and sweep. You may want to try to lay out a paradox of life that can be better expressed in a concrete example than in a clear "Subject" line. That requires reach, scope, and inspiration, not clipped clarity. Getting older is about discovering that things are rarely as simple as they seemed when you were 12.

20. Stepping off the path

The tightly controlled situations where you know exactly what to do because they're codified are few and far between when compared with the many more unclear situations the world consists of. They're pathways through the wilderness: there's a lot more not covered by them than the area they do cover. They're what Bill can help you with.

There's a reason to warn against drifting off the path as a result of not paying attention to where you put your feet. Most people who drift off unawares merely end up making what we call mistakes. You probably just end up in the bush, lost. Yet if you set off to leave the path with a purpose, you may discover new territory and map it for those who have never been there. Those who do so are our poets, travelers, and visionaries, or original writers: they've found something new that works. They extend the pathways of the possible. The problem therefore is not failing to stay on the path; it's failing to stay on the path and going nowhere. For most people, it's better to stay on the path. However if you think you know what you're doing in getting off the path, try it.

21. Bending rules

In any communication situation you can identify what the things are you absolutely have to do. These are expressed in rules. In a wedding ceremony, you have to say "I do" (or not say it); there's no other alternative. Most situations aren't this hide-bound. There's more room for choice, but it's always a choice among appropriate possibilities. If someone asks "What's new?" some things are appropriate and some things aren't: giving a lecture on trains isn't, but talking about your children or your job is. But nobody cares which of the appropriate things you choose. Thinking of Bill helps you distinguish what you have to do from what you get to choose, and helps make sure that what you choose is appropriate. To find out how far you can stray from the rules, you identify the particular Bill. Are you writing a Naval Academy memo? Are you answering a social question? Are you getting married? Are you trying to impress a date? Knowing how tightly determined a situation is determines what you say.

22. Moo

You have to look at the situation to see what works. You should always start by identifying the default—what's in bounds and what's out of bounds. But once you do that you're free to roam in the undetermined area, however large that is.

Here's a visual example of something that does "work" but so nearly doesn't we're conscious of the squeak-by. One day I noticed a pickup truck parked across from my office. I was on top of it, walking, before I realized it had been spray-painted in blotches. At first, from my perspective, the blotches looked like a bad spray job around rust. Then I realized they were all over the truck, and that they were white on black. I thought: *that's just like a cow*. Then I noticed the longhorns on the front of the hood. The pickup was *trying* to look like a cow! It was cute. But if the colors hadn't been black and white, and if the horns hadn't been on the dashboard, the truck would merely have looked like a sloppily spray-painted pick-up.

Here's a joke that doesn't work. My daughter saw a Cooper Mini. Suddenly she announced that the car up ahead was the perfect car for Disneyland. "Because it's so small?" I asked. "No," she said, puzzled I hadn't gotten her joke. "Mini, Minnie Mouse. You know. Get it?"

"Hah," I said.

She had to explain it, and it still wasn't a good joke. Most people won't get from the written word "Mini," clearly referring to this egregiously small car, to the homonym "Minnie," as in "Mouse." My daughter was working the connection from the wrong direction: she is fond of cartoons, so Minnie Mouse was pretty close to the surface of her consciousness. Being already at "Minnie Mouse" herself as a result of seeing a "Mini," she assumed Bill would get there from the car too. She misjudged the Bill. For most adults, there are just too many trails off "mini" to make it likely Bill would choose "Minnie Mouse" without further guidance. Maybe if somebody put huge ears on the car, the way somebody had put horns on the spotted truck, we'd make the connection.

Something that "works" does so because it's been set up so that Bill will naturally follow in the direction the writer had in mind. I don't think anyone would fail to get the direction of this pick-up truck toward "being" a cow once they saw the horns, because enough signposts were provided. The written word "Mini" on a car probably won't lead most people (adults?) to the homonym "Minnie" and from there to Disneyland. A lot of writing by wobbly writers assumes that Bill is where the writer is, rather than thinking about how to get him there. The writing is the providing of guideposts. That's what the work consists of: it positions things correctly for Bill. Thus writing has to decide what to include and what to exclude.

Good writing cuts channels so deep the water has to flow here, and nowhere else. Bad writing puts scratches on the surface, and then can't understand why the water goes all over.

23. *Photographs*

The passport photograph is to photography as Strunk and White writing is to writing. Sometimes that's just the kind of photograph you need. The trick is to be able to do other things (landscapes, still lifes, abstracts) without merely failing to do a successful passport photo.

We all know what it's like to mess up a family picture: someone moves, or is cut off, or the lighting is strange. Mere missteps from the path remain errors. To get something else you have to find a place that's far enough away it doesn't merely seem an error, yet close enough it's not unrelated to what we recognize as the default. A picture of a headless torso at least reminds us of the more standard shot it was probably intended to be. Some flubs are so interesting they become the equivalent of purposely missing the target's bull's-eye: snapshots that cut off people's heads have their own surreal charm. Museums sell books of bad postcards, boring photos of forlorn motels by deserted highways or empty lunchrooms, largely from the 1950s, whose creators had no idea one day they'd be seen as so bad they're good. But it's the person who collects them who makes the artistic statement, and can only do this by collecting a lot of them. Arguably the artist isn't the photographer who made the shot, but the one who saw them as bad and displayed them for that reason.

Yet most photographs aren't so bad they're good, they're junk or don't exist at all. Really bad photos are the royalty of bad photos; most are just mistakes, which then give way on the spectrum to photographs not taken at all. Most of life isn't individual enough for us even to bother snapping its picture. Think of the motions of tree leaves in the breeze, or the pattern of stones in your driveway, the patterns of clouds, or the ripples of water. We glance at these, and away: the variations are too small and too numerous for us to see any way to follow them. Or we may stare, mesmerized, overwhelmed at all these tiny things so different and yet so alike that, collectively, mean nothing at all.

24. 4'2"

The composer and theorist John Cage made a career out of taking bits of formless things and framing them so that we paid attention to them. One of his compositions (or as some might write it to show skepticism, "compositions") consists of the written command that several radios be tuned to whatever radio stations are available in the city the work is being performed in. Probably Cage's most famous composition (or perhaps you'll prefer "composition" once you know what it is) requires a pianist in full evening clothes to come out to the piano, dust the keys, and sit in silence for exactly four minutes and twenty-two seconds. It's called *4'2"*.

Those quotation marks around "composition" in the parentheses above are what we sometimes call "scare quotes," and they're meant to cast doubt that the thing really is what its name implies, or to show that the writer knows they're technical term not in common usage or a funny expression. (As an example of the last: "He's a 'squatter,' as we call someone living in a house without permission."—note that if you have quotes within quotes, or these within other quotes, you alternate single quotes with double so Bill can follow the relationships.) Some people think such quotation marks only serve to emphasize, so you'll get people using them instead of italics: "I thought he was really 'good.'" Does that mean he's not good? It's unclear what it does mean.

One piece like *4'2"* is a good idea (not a "good" idea). Think of how, sitting in silence expecting the pianist to start playing, we become conscious of other sounds that normally escape us: the hum of the air conditioning, coughs, perhaps titters as people "get it," or whispered asides, the squeak of chairs. But it couldn't be followed by another piece like this that lasts four minutes and twenty-*three* seconds. We can't listen to the radio piece for more than a time or two without getting bored: okay, we get it. Now what? But how many times can you read *Othello*? Lots. The point of Cage is to show us the world off the pathway is there, not to have us be intrinsically interested in it all. If so, our interest is collective, not specific, as it might be in the case of a newly-mapped territory.

25. Because he was Faulkner

Students sometimes ask me, "Sir, how come Faulkner can get away with not being clear and we can't?" The answer they think I'm going to give is an appeal to authority: they're just plebes, nobodies, and he's the very famous William Faulkner, a literary celebrity. RHIP (Rank Has Its Privileges).

Plebes who want to know why they can't write like Faulkner have failed to see that the style isn't the end for Faulkner, it's a means. Few plebes will have the thoughts of the scope and scale that require expression in Faulkneresque prose. And if they do, they won't end up being expressed in the same way. Derivative writers whose prose reeks of Writer X or Writer Y aren't producing the prose as a way of expressing a point of view, they're working from the opposite direction, toward something that already exists: they're copying a style, not creating it to express something else.

Faulkner didn't write letters the way he wrote novels. And when he worked in the post office he didn't spout "Faulkner" at the customers. He just sold them a stamp.

26. E.I.

Most plebes have never seen lower than a B+ grade on an English paper in their lives. Their writing was only part of a larger whole, which included their physical presence and personalities. The teacher added, consciously or unconsciously, what was missing from their papers, getting enough to feel vaguely satisfied, if not really nourished. Once students leave the more personal world of adolescence and high school, writing has to succeed on its own terms, without the personality. Writing isn't part of a larger whole that Bill gets; it's the whole thing. It's like a message put in a bottle and thrown out to sea. Suddenly it has to do all the work by itself. Frequently it doesn't. When this happens, I have to explain to them why it doesn't.

At the Naval Academy, coming by for help from a professor is called "getting E.I." E.I. stands for "Extra Instruction." In an E.I. session, the midshipman comes in, sits when invited to do so, and outlines the problem. Usually the problem is the fact that a paper has been turned back covered with markings and with a D or F at the bottom. If the midshipman understands my comments after looking at them, typically that's the last I hear of it. If the midshipman is here in my office, it usually means s/he has no idea why it received this grade. "I spent a lot of time on this paper, sir," s/he says.

If it got that low a grade, that's probably because it ends in a different place than it begins, is so full of mid-level errors I couldn't scrape up the willingness to continue, or never seems to have a thesis to begin with. I turn it over on my desk and say, "Tell me what your point was."

What comes out of the midshipman's mouth is always far more comprehensible than what's on the paper. Almost inevitably, first of all, I hear a clear main point. Sometimes I have to prompt them after that: "And your reason for saying that is—?" They're usually able to give me some justification of their position.

I hand the paper back to them. I ask, for what feels like the thousandth time in my teaching career: "Where on the paper does it say that?"

They scan the paper eagerly. After all, they came in thinking it was just fine. The answer has to be there somewhere; I've just missed it. Within seconds their eagerness flags, then turns to chagrin. "Nowhere," they admit ruefully. Reading the paper after they have actually had to formulate their point gives them new eyes.

The point was in their heads. It just didn't make it to the paper. However if it's not on the paper it doesn't exist for Bill.

Midshipmen, like many wobbly writers, typically don't really see that the squiggles they put on the paper are going to be translated by someone else. They're like cooks who've never understood any more than intellectually that somebody actually eats what they put on the plate.

Sometimes I say, "Let's Bill this paper."

To Bill a paper means, read it out loud to them, starting from the top, so they can see how the strokes the printer has left on the white surface will be translated by a reader. Readers read a piece of writing in the order in which the words occur on the page. The reader is compelled to go where the writer leads, or does not lead, him or her. The reader is like a rat compelled to follow a complicated series of passageways set up by the people in the white coats. Unlike the rat, however, the reader can always put down the writing, the rat's equivalent of jumping over the wall—which is probably what laboratory rats dream of because they can never hope to actually do it.

Wobbly writers don't seem aware that they are compelling someone to follow a specific pathway, so if the pathway is confusing, wandering, repetitive, or without a clear end, the experience will be frustrating to the person following. If it's too frustrating, the rat will jump the wall and go on its way.

"Billing" a piece of writing is almost always a revelatory experience for midshipmen: it makes them take the journey they had set up for Bill, see their own work through his eyes. Apparently they had never thought that Bill would be confused if they start on one topic and are shortly onto another. Or that Bill would be thrown off course as a result of their using a word that merely begins with the same letter as the one that they should have used. Or that Bill would have no idea how they got from their first point to the second. Or be confused by their using (say) a semi-colon, which is used to create a medium-length break, where they should have used a comma. [An example of such a mistake, with the sentence just above: "Or by using a semi-colon, which is used to create a medium-length break; where they should have used a comma." Bill says: Why is this writer breaking apart these elements that actually belong together? It's like seeing a person whose limbs float a few inches away from the torso. You can still tell it's a person, but you have to stop and scratch your head.]

II
Follow These Principles

1. Don't block the tube

You're Bill's only source of air. Don't put your finger over the tube.

Imagine Bill like Harry Houdini, the famous escape artist of the late nineteenth century and early twentieth century. Houdini liked to do things like having himself buried alive in chains in a sealed coffin and escaping. (Apparently the trick was tensing his muscles beforehand to give himself wiggle room with the chains.) Bill is buried alive. Only he's not Houdini, so he has an air tube. You have to maintain the air tube. If you put your finger over the tube, Bill can't breathe. You decide if he lives or dies.

Writing, similarly, is like talking to a computer: some mistakes look small to you but cause Bill major consternation, such as confusing "they're" with "their." To Bill it seems as if you don't know the difference between a contraction and a possessive. To you it's nothing, "one silly mistake." But if you get a single letter wrong in an e-mail address, it won't go through: to the computer it's the difference between getting through and having your mail returned.

The importance of something isn't determined by its size: a single screw missing in the wrong place of an airplane can cause a crash. If you give yourself credit for getting most of the airplane there, you're not seeing it from the mechanic's perspective. If you think you've done well to fill a page without asking what you've filled it with, you are thinking like yourself (Look!! I filled up a page!) and not like Bill, who gives you no credit for filling a page.

For some things, Bill has self-correction software built in, the way we're often re-directed from a mis-spelled Web site to the one we want (or maybe we get sent to a page set up to capture that particular error for its own purposes). Though disgusted by your confusion of "their" and "they're," Bill probably reads on. If you tell Bill you were "literally bowled over" Bill merely rolls his eyes; he knows that today many people think "literally" means merely "very" rather than "non-metaphorically." You've actually said a bowling ball knocked you down with the other pins, but probably you meant to say you were extremely surprised. Still, he can re-direct your mistake.

Similarly, Bill may forgive you not knowing that "conversely" isn't the same as "by contrast"; he may well forgive you if you jump from giving the positive aspect of your proposition to the negative without a transition such as "on the other hand." For a moment Bill is lost, then recovers: even after mis-cues like these, he probably corrects your mistakes and continues. But just because a mistake doesn't kill Bill doesn't mean he fails to notice it. And he's lost time and efficiency: the machine is coughing and sputtering, even if it hasn't stopped working altogether. Each interruption of the air in the tube blocks things for a second or two. If you interrupt Bill's breathing often enough by blocking the tube, he'll begin to panic and hyperventilate. Then he'll walk.

Sometimes I do too. When I can't take it any more, I merely draw a line in the middle of page two of a student paper and write: "I stopped correcting here." I'm not doing them a favor by taking anything they dish out. Bill won't.

2. Prepare for inspection

Writing is an alpha-level (most rigorous) inspection.

When you write, you should imagine that your uniform has just come from the cleaners and your creases are sharp, your ribbons are in the right order (there's a right and a wrong order) on your chest, your nametag is the proper distance from your pocket, you've "taped off" specks of dust on your uniform by wrapping masking tape around your fingers the sticky side out and patting yourself with the loop, and your shirt tuck is impeccable. You're making the very best impression you can. Then you look at yourself in the mirror to see how the officer in charge of the inspection will see you, which is not necessarily the same thing as how it feels to you.

It doesn't matter how long it takes you to get ready for an inspection or what it takes you to be ready. Perhaps it will take you more time and effort than your roommate, who's just neater or faster. But whatever the amount of time it takes to achieve the goal, that's the amount of time you invest. No one is interested, except perhaps your mother and, in a late night gripe session, your roommates, in how long it took you or what you had to go through to achieve it.

3. Be like Michelangelo

Michelangelo conceived of making a statue as merely removing the things that bound the figure in the stone. Sculpting was knowing what should be there, and then getting rid of the things that shouldn't be there. *Bill the Goat's Adult Refresher Guide to Writing* wants to help you eliminate all the parts holding the statue in the block of marble. That means, show you how to identify all the ways you can do wrong. But this means, you have to work on defining what the statue is supposed to look like so that when you've removed the last error, the last piece of stone holding it in, you can say: it's finished. You know what you're aiming at, or at least you know when you've gotten it. You have to think in terms of purpose.

The main reason for learning to think in terms of purpose, however, is that the purpose will vary from situation to situation. That means, the shape of the statue, what you write, will vary from case to case.

4. Fill the hole

Writing for Bill is like filling a hole that somebody else has already dug. The shape of the solid land you're required to fill will determine what you have to put in the hole. Despite the fact that this is *Bill the Goat's Guide Adult Refresher Guide to Writing*, Bill needs you to know that actually, there is no such thing as merely "writing," in the general. Writing is always a specific action, under specific circumstances, for a specific situation. This is true even if you're sitting down to write a poem you don't know anyone else will ever read. That's a specific situation too.

5. Make sure it's the right size

You only tell Bill what he needs to know. That means, you don't waste his time telling him what he does know.

So ask yourself these questions: What does Bill already know and what do I have to tell him? What is the shape of the hole I'm trying to fill? What he knows and what he doesn't determines the content of what you write, as it would determine the content of what you'd say to Bill if he were standing in front of you.

Midshipmen like to begin papers about a specific poem by Shakespeare with statements like this: "Mankind has always been interested in life-or-death questions." It may be true, but Bill is sure to know something that's this general. Besides, this could be the beginning of a thousand papers, not just this one. It's so generally true you can't move from something that huge to something as specific as a single poem inside of a normal-length paper. As a writer, you've misjudged the size of your hole. You don't begin a book on tactics in amphibious warfare with philosophical questions about whether or not war is intrinsically immoral. A book that does raise these issues will never get to the level of specificity of talking about the how-tos of amphibious warfare.

Deciding how large a hole you have to fill is comparable to similar decisions you make in the world every day that determines what you include and what you don't. What you tell people is determined by knowing who knows what, and what it's appropriate to tell them. You don't refer merely to "Sarah," your daughter, if you're talking to someone you've just met. You mention Sarah, then quickly identify her as being your daughter.

But that's not the only thing that's determined by reminding yourself what your interlocutor knows. Having just met the person you're talking to also determines what you say about Sarah. You may mention Sarah, because questions about children and marriage status are standard first-meeting questions. But if so, you'll probably stick to the fact that she exists and perhaps give her age. You don't go into her favorite color or current boyfriend.

Knowing who your Bill is determines what's appropriate for you to say. You can't read a specialist paper on Mayan temples to people who don't know what archaeology is. You tell them what archeology is, and use Mayan temples as one example. But you'll never be able to get to what makes Mayan temples, or this discovery about them, different: you have to emphasize what makes them typical of archeology. At most you can quickly mention one or two exceptions near the end.

Another example. One day, there was water on the deck in the weight room of the Aegis cruiser I was a guest on. The skipper wanted to know why. One of the Ensigns, such as my students become when they graduate and go into the Navy, had to find out and write him a report.

If Bill is your ship's C.O. you know he knows that there is a weight room on his Aegis cruiser. So you don't tell him that. Probably the C.O. even knows there is water on the deck, so you merely refer to that at the beginning of your report. Maybe you even cut right to the reason there's water on the deck.

But you can report this same incident to another Bill. That changes not just how you say it, but what you say. Writing isn't something that can be stripped from content, or something added to the content. Writing *is* content. What you say is part of the same spectrum of decisions as how you say it.

If Bill is your mother, she probably knows you're on an Aegis cruiser, but may not know there's a weight room. You have to start by telling her: "Dear Mom, Here's what's new in my life. Our ship has a small weight room. Last week it began to draw water." And so on. If it's to somebody who doesn't even know you're in the Navy, you have to say that too: "Dear John, Gee, we had some great times back in high school, didn't we? You may remember I went to the Naval Academy and graduated last year. Now I'm a J.O. [junior officer; you can use jargon, insider language or here, abbreviations, but you have to explain it to people who aren't familiar with it] on an Aegis cruiser [you'll have to explain that; John probably doesn't know]. Last week I had to write a report" and so on.

This example is still strange because it's unlikely you'd be able to make the leap from someone you knew back in high school but haven't talked to in years to the water on the weight room floor. If you wrote at all, it would be to re-establish the acquaintance, not to talk about water on the floor.

In this case the hole you're trying to fill is probably too big for what you're trying to fill it with. You need to address the fact of not having been in contact for years; it's unlikely you're going to be able to get to such a small issue as the water on the floor of the weight room in the same piece of writing.

Conversely, you can start too small. A paper about the Naval Academy full of its ubiquitous nautical jargon (a floor is a "deck," the toilets are the "head," a bed is a "rack" and so on) aimed at someone outside the Wall that surrounds our campus ("The Yard") is filling in a hole imagined to be smaller than the one you actually have.

6. Deal with the monster in your room

I tell midshipmen: If you burst into your company officer's room panting "Sir/Ma'am, it's got six!" your company officer will surely say: "Calm down! Six *what*? What is it? What's it doing?"

Instead, you need to burst into the company officer's room and yell: "Sir/Ma'am, There's a twelve-foot high monster in my room with six huge paws! It climbed in through the window! It just ate Mr. Parsons, my roommate, and now I'm afraid it's going to eat me!"

That is putting things in the order in which they need to be put. You determine the size of the hole you have to fill (you don't have to explain the concept of room, or roommate) and start there, neither with a larger nor a smaller hole than the one you should be filling.

However if you've broken your mother's favorite Chinese vase and want to write a little note to your mother about it before you go out in hopes of avoiding the storm, you'd probably be ill advised to begin "Mom, I broke the Chinese vase." It might instead be this: "Mom, I thought you'd like to know I already know what I'm going to get you for a birthday present. I'm going to buy you a Chinese vase just like the one in the family room. I know you'll say, 'But we don't need a second one.' True. But the fact is, as of about five minutes ago we don't even have a first one. At least, not a whole, not-in-pieces first one. Its remains are in the trash can. Apologies."

7. Know what your most important point is

You have to know what your most important point is, even if the form of writing you're doing (say, a novel, or a note to Mom) means you don't put it at the beginning. If it's appropriate, put off saying it: what you can't do is wander around.

A piece of writing loses a lot of points for a murky beginning, or one that flounders before it finds its course: beginnings count double, just the way first impressions do. It loses a lot of points for an ending that's not where Bill was expecting it to be. It loses a lot of points for jumping around, doing point One, then Two and Three, then back to Two, then adding to One. You have to organize your thoughts so that all of One, which is necessary to Two, is treated first, and then all Two, which is necessary to Three.

8. Don't be coy

Don't tease Bill. Don't flash an idea at him and make him wait until the next paragraph for you really to show it to him. Show it to him the first time, even if that's a paragraph later "But sir," my students say to this one, "I want to get him interested!" You haven't got Bill interested, you've annoyed him. The writer has presupposed that Bill will follow indefinitely. But Bill won't.

Adolescents think that anything they do is interesting to an outsider merely because they're doing it. After all, Mommy and Daddy think they're cute. Maturity is realizing that Bill isn't Mommy and Daddy. You have to constantly justify Bill's interest. He has other things to do.

Readers are the horses with blinkers over their eyes that see only the pavement as it unrolls; they can't look up. Wobbly writers fail to realize how helpless Bill is, condemned to process only the pavement he sees beneath his feet. You can frustrate him very easily. Don't.

9. Don't frustrate Bill

Bill has agreed to go for a run with you, the writer. Because it's your writing, you get to set the pace and the route. So you'd better make sure you've set a pace that's good for Bill, and not just for you, and you'd better make sure the route isn't full of meanders and dead ends. Don't change your course abruptly, or announce that you were wrong about the course. Don't continually kick Bill in the shins. **IF YOU FRUSTRATE OR INJURE BILL HE WILL NOT RUN WITH YOU.**

There are many ways of frustrating and injuring Bill, and injuries and frustrations come in many degrees. Small injuries are things like the writer thinking that "its" = "it's." Big frustrations are Bill having read the first paragraph of your piece and having no idea where you're going with it or what your main point is. Or getting to the end and finding out that your conclusion isn't what you said it was going to be back in paragraph one. Apparently you've changed your mind, but forgot to note that.

I tell students that every paper they turn in begins with a numerical grade of 100 and loses points as Bill reads. Bill starts off with goodwill, which fades as you hurt and upset him. All Bill notices is the loss from 100%.

If you plot your course well and give Bill a good run. Bill thanks you for the run, not for the preparation. However if you alienate Bill, you hear all about the things you did wrong. In a similar way, your reward for keeping your wits about you as you go about your daily routine, say driving to and from work, is that you stay alive and get to do what you were on your way to do without ending up dead or in the hospital.

Writing well is like wearing flattering clothing: if you pick the right clothes, it's you people notice rather than the clothes. But if you pick the wrong ones, the clothes become the topic of conversation.

10. Make your course clear in advance

Always give Bill as much warning regarding what's coming in the course you're running together as you can. If you're laying out four pieces of evidence pointing to a single conclusion, give him the conclusion first, then the evidence, not the reverse. If you're giving arguments both pro and con something but ultimately choose the pro side, make that clear at the beginning, not the end. If you refer to "the most important X" or "a major Y" tell Bill immediately what X and Y are. Don't make him beg, and don't tantalize him.

When riding a horse, the rider turns his or her head in the direction s/he wants to go. The horse senses the shift in weight and is ready to go in that direction; the rider stays in the saddle. If you change course or loop with Bill running at your side, he trips or at least begins to grumble: "Where the heck are you taking me?"

Don't make Bill have to ask. And make very sure he doesn't ask in an annoyed tone of voice. Instead take care of all this beforehand. Tell Bill where you're going to go, and then go there.

If you have surprising, or troubling, or extremely positive news, you prepare it as much as possible. You say where you're going: "The following data may prove troubling for some listeners." "We reached the following stunning conclusions." If you're talking to your roommate, you may very well be able to slip a surprise in without preparing it: you'll be there to deal with the reaction. In the case of a horror movie, the audience would be disappointed if it were *not* surprised and shocked. But that's precisely what they're prepared for.

A novel or short story consists to a large degree of precisely this buffering of information. "Creative writing" sets up a one-of-a-kind situation, that all has to be explained to us: who are these people? Where are they? Why are they here? Nobody knows these things because they're made up: we have no information for them. Creative writing is as much about eating food as a memo is, but it also includes all the preparations and background, as a memo does not. It's a picnic, not a quick lunch in the cafeteria: it's not only allowed but necessary to set up the tablecloth, plates, glasses, and silverware before the food is taken out.

11. Say it once

In informal speech, people hesitate, start again, make mistakes and go over the same territory, and repeat themselves. In writing all that's just annoying, unless the purpose is precisely to make us aware of the cadences of spoken speech. Playwrights like David Mamet and Sam Shepard are known for rendering many of the re-starts and repetitions of real speech in a form that forces us to be aware of them. Here that doesn't obscure the content, because this *is* the content. That's rarely true elsewhere.

Because the reader can go back over what's on the page, errors that pass unnoticed in hearing, as a single time, become glaring when looked at twice or three times. It's the same way an error in a recording can annoy us on repeated listenings—which is why so much time is spent on making recordings flawless.

If you change your mind in writing, you don't suddenly say in the middle of page three that oh yes, you've changed your mind, but by going back to the top of page one and making sure what's there reflects the change. If you say it multiple times, be aware you're doing it, and flag it as a repetition to Bill. Perhaps it's emphasis, or it's summary, or it's so important it has to be said again. Or perhaps it's your main idea, and each time you bring it up you add something to it and expand on earlier points: be clear with Bill that that's what you're doing. Just don't act (or worse, be) unaware of the repetition.

The correlate of "say it once" in written works is that you have to set things up so Bill sees it's something he needs to pay attention to when he reads it. Setting things up properly so Bill gets your point the first time around is what allows you to say it only once. Some of the ways you can set things up so Bill pays attention are by putting your point at the top of the paper or the paragraph, giving it its own sentence, or preparing it with a tag: "The most important issue here is ..."

12. Get the level of importance right

Many injuries to Bill are caused by writers not giving clear signs of the level of importance of their points. Decide how important each point is, and give it the proper weighting. Don't make too much of small things; don't make too little of big things. (This is a rule for verbal communication as well.) If you prepare Bill for a bombshell and drop a pin, he'll be annoyed. Similarly, if you make an incendiary remark or surprising claim as an aside, in a parenthetical expression, or in the middle of the paragraph, Bill thinks you don't realize how important it actually is. This may be the way it occurred to you when you were writing. But part of writing is correctly assessing what your shovel turns up and bringing it to prominence.

There are many ways to signal importance level. Getting the signals correct isn't something you add to writing, it *is* writing. Signals include including or not including phrases, positioning, and punctuation. All of them are in your tool box, and as you write all have to be available.

13. Know the difference between writing time and your time

The progress of time in a piece of writing is internal to the writing, Bill's world. It's not measured by the time in your world. You may have sat before a blank computer screen for a long time, had snacks, tried several times to figure out your own point, and re-organized things over and over. None of this should make it to the paper.

Bill doesn't usually care what conclusion you've come to; he just wants you to be clear to him about what it is. It's not cheating to change your opening if you figure out what your point is halfway through your first version. The trick is to make it look as if that's where you wanted to go all the time.

14. Anticipate reactions

One of the best ways you can smooth the way for Bill, make him continue to run with you, is to anticipate his reactions and respond to them. This is an element of writing that is found in verbal communication as well. Many reactions are anticipated in the very process of putting words on the page, say in the structure of the sentences: the writer turns things around as s/he puts them on the page so that they fall in the best position, or senses things getting out of hand as s/he writes and fixes the problem immediately.

Here's a sentence I included in an early draft of *Bill's Guide*: "There's a world of difference between, on one hand, knowing what the most important thing is and deciding on a different order for a reason you either know or intuit (some things don't have to be articulated to be clear, such as that your spouse is angry with you: you just know) and, on the other, not knowing what the most important thing is, or knowing but simply refusing to give it for no visible reason." It's comprehensible, but it's certainly on the edge of having so much in it as to be incomprehensible. My first version of the sentence was even worse. It began "There's a world of difference between knowing what" and so on—I got through the end of the parenthetical before I realized I'd gone on so long no one would be able to follow it. So, without having finished the sentence, I went back to the beginning and inserted the "flag" "on one hand" which makes the reader aware that what follows is half of a comparison. It's a visible enough flag I can even permit myself to add a parenthetical. That in turn determined that when I continued after the parenthetical I had to put the second half of the flag pair, "on the other." Even so, there were so many elements in the sentence it was difficult to follow. Finally, even after all that fixing, I decided it didn't pass the test of being Bill-friendly, so I cut it. That's anticipating reactions too.

What you cut out of a written piece is as much a decision regarding your Bill as what you put in. Not including something determines a written work as much as including it. Many things fail to be included because they're never proposed—we have the knack of not wasting time on the completely inappropriate—or are rejected in a second or two, or the second time through. You don't have to justify the assertion that cats and dogs are domestic animals; nobody will disagree (unless your Bill lives somewhere where this isn't the case). You don't have to explain about refrigerators (everybody knows: unless Bill doesn't). You don't have to talk about why people eat (Bill knows; goats eat for the same reasons—unless your reasons are beyond the norm for goats, or most people).

The computer programs that preserve every keystroke of the writing process, should someone have the dogged patience to follow a read-out of someone composing on the keyboard, would be full of words changed, commas put in and taken out, sentences begun again, and countless decisions that are made in the process of writing. They come thick and fast. In the same way that identifying the solid rim of the hole you're trying to fill and starting there becomes the body of your writing (do I have to tell Bill that there is a U.S. Naval Academy and that first-year students there are called "plebes" or can I merely begin with "Plebes do X and Y"?), so too anticipating objections *is* your writing.

At the same time, you have to anticipate Bill's reaction to your assertions. If you make an assertion that very few people agree with, your Bill had better be a group of those people. Otherwise, part of your writing has to be an immediate laying out of evidence. If you refer to Adolf Hitler as "one of the twentieth-centuries worst murderers," you can probably put this in an aside. All but a very few people share this view. If you refer to a U.S. President this way, and your book is not for readers of the far left, prepare immediately to defend it. Better is, prepare Bill for the statement before you give it, perhaps as follows: "Though few people would accept a comparison between Adolf Hitler and any U.S. President, in certain isolated qualities President X did have something in common with the German mass murderer." Then you go on to make your point. Or perhaps you decide the point simply cannot be made without a storm of protest that would drown out your argument. This happens again and again in political discourse where a U.S. leader or institution is compared for dramatic effect one of the arch-villains of history. It never works in speech, buffer it though you may. It might work in the cooler medium of writing, but I still would say it's not worth the trouble. Find another way of saying what you have to say.

15. *Don't mountain-top*

From your position as writer, you can imagine the whole terrain of your argument as if on a topographical map; you oversee the whole. Thus many writers fall into the habit of "mountain-topping," which is jumping from the tip of one point to the tip of the next point.

The problem is that Bill doesn't see things from your point of view. He can't jump from mountain to mountain; he's got to plod down one mountain and up the next. He can't jump from peak to peak. He's not a mountain-goat; in fact he lived on the Naval Academy dairy farm with the cows, until it was sold. (Here I anticipate the reader, who can't be Bill in this particular case, will ask: where does Bill live now? Answer: I don't know.)

"But," the wobbly writer replies, his or her feelings hurt. "Doesn't he trust me? All Bill has to do is follow me! I know where I'm going!"

The world is full of people who claim they know what they're doing and don't. Bill has long ago learned to be suspicious. So you have to win his trust. You can't do this if you give him shorthand versions of things and don't bother to explain how you arrived at your conclusions.

16. Know what the deal-breakers are

If midshipmen show up for inspection wearing the wrong uniform, they will be "flamed on" (yelled at: how could you have been so stupid? What kind of a dirtbag are you? etc.) and sent back immediately to change, as well as being punished with a certain number of demerits. In order to take part in the exercise you have to showing wearing the correct uniform. That's a precondition. It's not negotiable.

Sometimes students say to me, "Okay sir. I see the mistakes. But did you like my main argument?" We're not even there, I tell them. You have to get the uniform right even to take part in the exercise.

The world is full of deal-breakers of this sort. You wear a tie to a job interview, if male, and, if female, something from Talbot's rather than Frederick's of Hollywood. Otherwise you'll be shown the door, no matter how much you know.

Knowing the deal-breakers means you might be able to negotiate them. If the first thing you (if male) say when you walk in to your job interview not wearing a tie is a hearty "I need to apologize for my not having a tie. The fact is, the flight was late and my luggage was lost. I had to hustle to get here," you may well get the job. You don't always have to adhere to the default, but you do have to be aware of it.

By acknowledging the default, what Bill expects, you can usually get him to accept doing something else. "Most people would say that the United States is X. However we should at least consider the possibility that it's Y—or even anti-X." If you just start in with the anti-X you have very little chance of convincing Bill of anything. It's as if you're telling him the sky isn't blue and up, but brown and down. It's possible to make the case that it is brown and down, but making the case is the body of what you have to say.

Being aware of divergences from the default and admitting them openly is a major skill in the game of being a successful adult. If you can be aware that (say) the woman you're trying to impress is looking away and acting impatient and you can identify the cause, you may be able to save the day after all. You say, "I'm afraid I haven't made a very good impression by doing X. I hope you'll forgive me, but in fact I'm a little distracted." It might work. If you realize that somebody is getting testy with you on the telephone, you identify what's happening: "I'm sorry, I'm finding it difficult to concentrate because it seems to me I'm making you impatient." The tone you hear may change.

You explain changes of plan the same way: "Normally we'd be doing X at this point. However because of A and B, instead we're going to do Y." This is important both with children, who expect things to happen in a very precise way, and for adults, who are aware of the social defaults. You identify the default and then explain the divergence: "Normally we'd go to the park but it's raining, so we're going to play inside instead."

With adults you do the same thing. If the room at a conference is too hot, you don't just pretend it isn't and try to ignore it. You say, "Ladies and Gentlemen, I have to apologize for the heat here in our meeting room. There has been a problem with the air conditioning that we're working on. I'll cut the remarks short and would encourage everyone to loosen ties and remove jackets." Acknowledging the situation may get people to smile and re-focus.

17. Understand the medium

Most of the problems people have with writing itself come from the fact that they don't understand the nature of the medium. If they did, they would work with it more confidently.

Actors go to classes to understand the stage; writers have to understand the page. Actors learn what things they do produce what effects in the audience. They have to learn the difference between talking normally and playing to the back balcony. And then stage actors learn by watching their own screen tests they have to tone down their gestures for the movie camera. Similarly, writers have to understand how the page is different than talking face to face.

When you speak, you add all the visual cues that can fill in the holes in what you're saying for the listener. On the page, stripped of things like your face, your expressions, tone of voice, and hand gestures, the holes become all too evident. There's nothing and no one to fill them in.

The reason people can get away with speaking this way is that so much of the slack is taken up with the other aspects of the situation. First among these is that we have another person in front of us, a real human being who isn't going to go away. We breathe the same air, occupy the same space. It's difficult to tune out lively people we want to hear who are very close to us and looking us in the eye. It's easiest to tune out people who are talking to us from far away, at the front of a large crowd, and speaking mechanically—say, by reading their remarks. What they have to say becomes more like writing.

The linguistic philosopher Jacques Derrida, who loved turning things on their head, made sport with the idea that verbal speech is more "here" than written speech. His claim seems at first glance counter-intuitive. Of *course* verbal speech is more "here" than written! If someone is talking to you, you're not likely to fall asleep, for starters. Yet Derrida is making a good point. When you read a book, it's just you and the book. You have absolute access to what's on the page, just as absolute as someone else a half a world away reading the same book. Each of you is alone with the page. When you hear someone talk, by contrast, the speech is still the speech of the living person. It still somehow belongs to the speaker, in a way the writing no longer belongs to the people who wrote it. They've put it in the bottle and thrown it in the ocean.

Of course a real person wrote the message in the bottle, not a machine. The sociologist and philosopher Michel Foucault made a lot of friends, and an equal number of enemies, by announcing that "the author" was dead. This caused many people to snort in derision, and many others to applaud. Foucault and Derrida collectively express the warm-cold nature of writing. Derrida emphasized the warm, Foucault the cold. Writing is warm because it's there in your hands, the book or the report. You have direct contact with the printed object. It's cold for precisely those reasons too: the real person behind it isn't there. Foucault was emphasizing that the link with the person behind it has dried up: the message has been put in the bottle, though once it was written by real hands. Both the author and his or her absence are aspects of writing.

The Anglo-American "New Critics" of the 1950s and beyond influenced several generations by insisting that we should look at the text rather than things like biography of the writer. This is the same as saying that in the case of writing, if it's not on the page, it's nowhere. But it remains true that the page was written by a person. Even today many people are made more comfortable with writing by having its personal origins emphasized. That's the reason for the immense popularity of biographies, including biographies of writers: we feel we're connecting with the real person. It's arguable that what brings us away from the text takes us away from the realest thing we have.

The world of the reader is not the world of the writer. The most fundamental difference is that the writer knows where the writing is going, or should, and the reader is condemned to figure it out, piece by piece by laboriously digested piece.

18. Ask, How's it going to look in print?

Many things people say in the heat of the moment that end up in print, usually in a newspaper, are figures of fun to people who read them in black and white. The person quoted never thought what s/he said would end up in the newspaper. The speed of speaking and the "add-on" factors mean they can get away with things verbally that won't pass muster in written form. Knowing what you say is going to be quoted could encourage to speak for Bill as well as write.

Writing for Bill could also reduce if other problems intrinsic in the transposition from verbal to written language. Aside from the homonym problems like "their/there/they're" or "it's/its," we have expressions that simply don't make sense when people write what they hear rather than asking what the expression means. I laughed out loud the first time I read on a student paper that this world of ours is a "doggy dog" world. The person said "dog eat dog" so quickly it sounded to him like "doggy dog" and had probably never seen it in print. I was amused recently at reading that something had "peeked" the writer's interest (peek=look at quickly or furtively; should have been "piqued"). If the writers realized that Bill would read this rather than hear it, they might write correctly. Is it "to give someone free rein" or "free reign"? The first, because it's a horse metaphor, not about a king.

19. Don't think like a midshipman

I have to say repeatedly to midshipmen, "Don't think like a midshipman." Midshipmen are taught to "sound off," to speak loudly and distinctly. Aggressiveness is prized. Being sure of yourself in public is its own reward.

This may work in person, but it doesn't work in the cooler medium of writing. The person reading your writing has pulled your message from the bottle. In writing, you can't shout Bill down. You actually have to convince him.

The saying has it that "revenge is a dish best eaten cold." Writing is a dish that almost inevitably *will* be eaten cold. Only rarely will writing have the "here and now, hot off the presses" quality of speech (say, a manifesto in the middle of a revolution). In writing, you have to put your money where your mouth is—immediately, without making Bill beg. You can't turn up the volume, because it's too easy for Bill to just hold the paper further away, or put it down, or laugh and throw it away. On the page, bombast shrivels to posturing.

Many midshipmen are under the misapprehension that an assertion is typically either all wrong or all right. They don't understand that life rarely is so clear, that instead what we typically do is defend our point of view as *more* plausible, *more* believable, *more* worthy of being adopted—not as correct and certainly not as self-evident. A good deal of the fabric of writing is explaining why the plausible you're defending is more plausible than others' plausibles. Thus you have to know where your point fits into the larger scheme of things. And make this clear.

20. Be clear in your references

You know the person you're referring to. Bill doesn't.

One of the major casualties in the transfer from speaking to writing is clarity regarding the people you're speaking/writing about. In speech, you interject explanations as you feel they're needed ("I mean the same man I was just talking about"). You can go back and clear up uncertainty, or your listener can ask: "You mean X or Y?"

If you write about "John," your buddy Bill has to know who John is: is it the man you were talking about last paragraph, the Evangelist, or your best friend? What Bill has to know about John, however, is determined by what you need him to know for your purposes. Sometimes "John" is just a random name that could well have been Mark or Joe. You have to make that clear too, say by using the word "say": "Let's take a man named, say, John."

Be consistent in your references. If you call somebody "The Man in the Yellow Hat," that's the way you have to refer to him the second and subsequent times—unless you're only talking about one man, in which case it becomes funny that you don't, after a time or two, merely call him "the man," or give him a name. In the Curious George books, making him merely "The Man in the Yellow Hat" is a way to cast the book from the monkey's perspective.

Pronouns are tricky. If you write "he" or "its," the reader had better be able to say immediately who "he" or "it" is. The same is true of "this." There's no rule telling you how to do this: you put yourself in Bill's position and decide. Does "he" clearly refer to someone you've already identified? Only one somebody? A somebody that Bill doesn't have to look too long for? If it was four sentences before, he has to look too long—but a single sentence might not be too long. It's a matter of timing, like giving the punch line in a joke: the fact that there's no hard and fast rule doesn't mean it isn't an issue. A text with nothing but "he" would be consistent in its own way too: it would be about someone whose name is irrelevant. That's information for Bill too.

21. Avoid clichés

At this point in time
Clear in your own mind
As regular as clockwork
As happy as a clam

All these are clichés. The grammar books tell us not to use them. Why not? They sound fine to most writers, even original.

The reason, here as always, is: Bill. You have to realize that to Bill, these will be boring because he's heard them so often. Of course he's heard the words "a," "and," and "the" often too, but these aren't trying to be different. Clichés are. Bill has very low expectations of "a" or "and." But if you use a turn of phrase that's not a sober-sides, it had better be good. You take a bigger hit for trying for more and failing than you do for settling for less to begin with. The default is never wrong: a white shirt to work may be boring, but it's always acceptable.

You may be able to use them if you acknowledge the default and thus show you know they're over-used. You can say, "I'm as happy as the proverbial clam." If you think Bill hasn't gotten your point, you can keep the joke going for a bit: "Though why clams should be thought to be happy is beyond me."

From this we see that there's no one right way to write or talk; people think of new ways all the time. Each way has to be judged on its own merits, like jokes. Some jokes are funny and some aren't; some are funny under certain circumstances and not under others; some are funny when told by one person and not by another. The same is true of language usage. There's no rule book that will give you an absolute guide to things that always work.

A cliché ("I'm happy a clam") may seem original to you because it's not the most usual expression ("I'm very happy"). But because it's the most frequent and obvious side-step from the beaten path, it's become its own sort of beaten path. A wobbly writer can see only that it's off the main path, so it seems original.

In the same way, you might think somebody's name is funny the first time you hear it. People need to be taught never to make fun of someone's name. You can be very sure that whatever joke you might make is something the person him- or herself has heard hundreds of times. You're trying for original, and all you get is a grimace and a reputation for insensitivity. Besides, there are few things more personal to the person who bears it than his or her name. So it's not an appropriate subject for jokes. You, hearing it the first time, might think it's funny. But you have to think of how Bill is going to react.

Being able to see your actions from others' point of view is the basis of good manners, what we call politeness. It's the grease that makes the social machine function.

22. Don't Ballpark

Here's an advertisement from the Internet for the luxury ($400 a night) Indian train "Palace on Wheels" that tours Rajasthan, the area in the northwest of India known for its maharajas and very old kingdoms. "The exquisite and exclusive Palace On Wheels has luxurious cabins, wall to wall carpeting, a well stocked bar, two dining cars and a very personalized service... in fact, almost everything that could compromise of heaven on earth for seven days!"

This contains a number of what Bill has to call mistakes. The worst is at the end: the writer doesn't know the difference between "compromise" and "comprise," neither of which works with "of."

I call such mistakes "ballparking," as in: anywhere in the ballpark is good enough. To you, the writer, any word that starts with "com" and has a "pr" in it is close enough to what you're looking for. You probably even think you've done a good job by coming up with a word that is sort-of what's called for. After all, you didn't say "anteater," or "supercilious," you said "compromise"—which as anyone can see is very close to "comprise." Don't you get credit for that?

Sure. It's just that what for you counts as specificity (it's close enough) is still so imprecise to Bill he's lost. The ball, granted, is in the ballpark. This isn't a clearly wrong place, like the parking lot or the shopping mall, so you're proud of yourself. But it's still not good enough. You want to hit the ball in a precise direction. Otherwise you don't get on base.

General Motors' sales and marketing vice president is quoted from the *Detroit News* (*Washington Post* June 11, 2005, A9) on the failure of a Pontiac car called the Aztek that nobody wanted to buy and the economic hit the company took on it. "The chapter is over. Japan Inc. passed us up. It's old news. Our mindset is—we've got to fight back." The speaker is not a politician surrounded by flaks and partisans eager to make him look like the Messiah, so pointing out he's got it wrong won't cause half the people out there to shoot out of their seats with indignation. I think we can say without causing a major storm: he got it wrong.

The worst mistake here is a ballpark one. The speaker knows he needs an expression with "passed." It's just that it's not what he offers, which is "passed up." To "pass up" something means refuse it when it's offered, or fail to take advantage of it. What he needs is just "passed." So our General Motors VP is uttering nonsense. There are other problems too: a "mind-set" is much more general than an attitude, which is what he's expressing by saying "we've got to fight back" and is the word he should have used. Besides, our speaker is mixing metaphors. He starts with a book and then goes (I think) to a race. The chapter is over, but they've been "passed."

Here's what he could have said: "The chapter is over. Japan Inc. wrote its end. That's all there is in that book. Our feeling is, we've got to write another book, a best-seller this time."

But sir, as my students say, didn't you understand it?

Yes: the error is only mid-to-lower level, so Bill isn't dead. He's just taken a couple of hits. But a couple of hits in so short a passage are a couple too many. It's taken Bill far too much time to do double-takes and fix the mistakes so he can stay on course.

In my first version of the paragraph with the quote, above, I wrote: "a Pontiac car nobody wanted to buy called the Aztek." It sounded fine to me when I wrote it, because I knew that it was the car that was called the Aztek, not "nobody wanted to buy." When I re-read it, I realized Bill would have to take precious split-seconds going over the sentence to be sure it was the car that was the Aztek, so I moved its elements around. Strunk and White tell you to get the modifiers close to the noun to prevent confusion; they don't try to get you to sense the confusion, which is what I'm doing here. If you sense the confusion, you have a greater motivation for preventing it.

Every day I correct the papers of the otherwise spit-and-polished 21-year-olds who "ballpark" in this way. Making these "ballpark" errors doesn't mean you're a bad person. It just means you're not thinking of Bill. Our General Motors man is presumably a highly competent professional. When his mistake is explained it seems evident. Why couldn't this man, presumably no dummy, say it correctly? Probably he wasn't thinking of Bill either. It's a common failing, but that doesn't mean it isn't a failing. Bill knows that readers of *Bill's Guide* probably make mistakes like this. But now let's talk about how to do it right.

I've found that people frequently know when they're ballparking. They get an uneasy feeling in the pit of their stomach but ignore it. They know they need a word that begins with "sp." Is it "specious" or "speculative"? They don't know, and they're not thinking of Bill's pain, so they don't bother to find out.

All midshipmen are issued a dictionary. Use it, I tell them. I bet there's a dictionary or two on Wall Street, and there are certainly dictionaries on your computer. Ignore that grammar check; it's mostly nonsense. It thinks like a machine, rather than like a person, and can't conceive of Bill. So it makes all sorts of ludicrous mistakes, and suggests things you might accept if you're not thinking of Bill. And spell check will only catch words that don't exist, not homonym switches like "they're/their" or ballparking problems. Being a functioning adult isn't about knowing all the answers. It's about knowing some answers and knowing where to get the rest. But you have to know the difference between what you have and what you need to get. You make this distinction by looking at where you are relative to where you need to be.

Not all ballparking mistakes will disappear if you go with your gut. The advertising campaign for a brand of gas sold in the mid-Atlantic region caused me to burst out laughing. Huge signs affixed to posts at gas stations trumpeted: "Quality is not an option."

Quality is not an option? That means that it's not possible to get quality with this gasoline. Is that really what they want to be admitting to customers?

The confusion of the sign-writer became clear when I saw the line underneath: "Expect it." This only made sense if the sign-writer thought that what s/he had said was that quality was not *optional*, something you had to ask for, but was instead a given, part of the package.

The distinction is thus between something being "an option" and being "optional." Somebody's head is going to roll for that one! I thought. I even considered the possibility that it was one of those purposely wrong signs that the consumer was supposed to remember for that reason. No: for that it wasn't clearly enough wrong. It was off the beaten path, but not in a new territory.

After a year or so, I noticed one day that the signs were still there. Maybe nobody's head had rolled after all? I sat down and wrote a letter to the president of the company. The president had his legal counsel write a funny/rueful letter back saying that yes, they had taken flak from many sources for this, including journalists. But as they'd invested so much money in the campaign and the signs, and gotten relatively few complaints, mostly from English professors and professional writers, the signs were going to stay. Sorry about that. And indeed, when I repeated this story to all of my students, not one could tell me what was wrong with the signs. By the same token, however, they couldn't tell me what it meant. They just hadn't paid attention. Maybe that's why so much bad writing gets by people? They just don't ask what it means!

Learn to notice things about language is like learning to notice things about social interactions. How do you know what's appropriate, what you have to do and where you have some room for choice? Just watch what others do who seem to know what they're doing. Noticing is like listening. People who like to hear themselves talk are sometimes deficient in it.

23. *Don't make statements that won't pass muster*

Another sort of writing problem doesn't say anything.

This, at any rate, is the way I initially wrote the above sentence. Bill doesn't read it the way I wrote it, however: to Bill, it's saying that the problem itself doesn't say anything. Clearly Bill needs to hear that the problem is a phrase/usage that doesn't say anything, so let's correct the sentence accordingly: Another sort of writing problem occurs when a phrase is used that isn't wrong, but just doesn't say anything.

That's still not good enough. "Doesn't say anything"? What does that mean? Really says *nothing*? No, that's not my point. Let's try again:

Another sort of writing problem occurs when a phrase is used that isn't wrong, but makes claims that don't stand up under scrutiny. In talk it may well pass muster, but it writing it won't.

That's better.

A sentence on a tourist map for the State of Maryland asserts of the Eastern Shore, where I grew up, that "The Eastern Shore is equal parts relaxation and excitement."

This is one of those cases where the writer didn't think enough about Bill. If you say something is "equal parts" that's quite mathematical, a very precise claim. So Bill wonders, why *equal* parts? Why not 60% and 40%? And for that matter, how can a place be *composed of* relaxation? And this: are we being told that these together make 100%? It's logically possible that it's only 1% of each, so that we wonder what the rest of it is.

It probably sounded good to the writer, but Bill is distracted by the unverified claims it makes. If you're only justified in making a statement that's at level 5 in precision on a 10-level scale, don't try for an 8 or 9. Stick with the 5. That way you don't leave Bill with the sense that you've claimed more than you can substantiate.

Much more to the point here would have been: "The Eastern Shore is both exciting and relaxing." That doesn't over-reach by getting into mathematical territory, and it makes clear that "is" is introducing qualities, not things of which it's composed.

If something is only mildly whatever, say that it's mildly whatever. Don't beat the drums and then make the unjustifiable assertion that it's completely whatever. Getting your knuckles rapped for an overreach is worse that merely asserting the more usual thing to begin with and moving on. Not everything is a 10. Many things are merely 5. Bill can accept that.

24. Stage public executions

One way to make clear that you both know what your point of view is and anticipate how Bill is going to react is to stage public executions of your opponent's best argument.

You say: "Opponents of my position will argue that so-and-so, but this is insufficient/simple-minded/wrong-headed for the following reasons." This lets you control an objection before the fact and makes your argument more plausible.

If you try this, you actually have to hit your opponent's strongest argument. If you pick a weaker one because it's easier for you to take down, you'll look silly and the stronger argument, when it is offered, will look that much stronger. It's like going hunting: if your shot goes astray you scare away the deer. It's worse than not shooting at all.

25. Showcase your best muscles

Come on strong with your best muscles, and don't apologize too much for your less impressive ones: mention them once and then move on. By the same token, you do have to acknowledge their weakness. That way you control the response to them. Timing and nuance are all-important here, as they are in speech. If you seem defensive, you may come off as "protesting too much"—claiming not to be affected by something that, by bringing it up and leaning on it, you show you're bothered by. Weak arguments come last, if at all, and then only as add-ons. Similarly, certainty comes before speculation: you're allowed to guess, but label it as possible rather than sure, and do it at the end. That way you control objections by keeping them down to a tolerable level. End of discussion, thank you very much and any questions please?

26. Don't overdrive your headlights

In driving classes, we're taught not to drive faster at night than our headlights allow. The headlights give a certain distance in which we can react. If we drive too fast we can't react to an emergency within this distance.

Bill is the headlights, condemned to a fixed absolute distance. The writer is the car that can go at any speed it wants. The writer can conceive of long strings of ideas that come out in great sweeps on the page. In order to get a complete idea, typically we have to finish a whole sentence, and then subsequently the whole paragraph. If there are too many things that have to be held in memory before Bill sees how they fall into place, he feels the car is going too fast for him. He's overdriven. Bill is overcome by nausea and panic: something bad is going to happen. Slow down.

27. Feed Baby Bill

Your writing voice is what you want Bill to be used to. When you quote, you introduce someone else's voice. If Bill is used to your voice, he'll initially have trouble concentrating on the other voice, especially if it goes on too long. This is the first problem with over-quotation. The subsequent danger is that he'll get to like the other voice better than yours. You can quote from other authors, but you have to do it in a controlled way.

You do it by feeding Baby Bill. Baby Bill sits in his high chair. You prepare him for the fact that the spoon is coming his way so he's got his mouth open. You say, "Mmmmm, squashed peas!" and you smack your own lips. Then you circle the spoon around his face.

You don't overload the spoon. If you put too much on, the squashed peas don't end up in Baby Bill's mouth, but on the floor instead. After Baby Bill has eaten his peas, you say, to reiterate, "Mmmm, good, squashed peas!"

Pare quotations down to the barest minimum, and then pare them some more. A few words inserted in the middle of your own sentence is best. If you can't avoid quoting full sentences, or even paragraphs, you retain control as follows: you tell Bill beforehand what the point is, and why you're quoting them. "From the GAO's newest report on the national debt we realize that [summary of the point X in the report that you're emphasizing]." Then you quote the report's passage on the debt that makes the points X in what will probably be a voice more difficult than yours for the reader to follow. Keep the GAO's report as short as possible. Then you take back the voice: "This shows us that ..." You have to make clear to Baby Bill that you have the power to give the GAO report, and you have the power to take away the GAO report. His job is merely to eat. After your quote, you reiterate the point again without repeating it. You don't want to end with some other writer buzzing in Bill's brain. Besides, you can probably say it clearer than the GAO report does.

28. Don't get too attached to your own words

Let's say you've identified the hole and filled it, thinking of Bill. You've established an internal, logical time in your writing which is determined by the relationship of your points, not by what you went through to make them. You've punctuated, inserted flags to indicate shifts, broken up or sewed together sentences to make clear the relationship of ideas and their relative importance. You've anticipated Bill's objections, acknowledged your unavoidable weaknesses, and publicly executed your opponent's best man.

You're done, you think. Think again. The next part is even harder. All those beautiful words on the page that may have cost you so much time and effort! They're your words, so you love them.

But they're not your words for you, they're for Bill. So you have to be hard-hearted. You have to push these beloved words out into the cold world. That's where they're soon going to be anyway, so you have to see if they can survive on their own.

Many wobbly writers hate revising. This is so because they don't know what they're looking for when they re-read. They're like those high school kids told to sit there for the next ten minutes and review the text. Most will simply kill the time, their eyes glassing over, the letters swimming before them. Being told to sit there and look until the teacher releases them feels sadistic to them. They're still in their own heads, not Bill's. It's a whole new world full of exciting discoveries if suddenly they ask not, How did this look to me (to which the answer is always: fine)? but, How does it look to Bill?

29. Revise

If you're working on a computer, print out the piece of writing. It's easier to catch problems on paper than it is on the endless flow of the computer screen.

Then you read it out loud to Bill: put Bill, or his substitute, on the chair in front of you. If you can bring yourself to do it, read it in a funny voice, so it doesn't sound like you. That way it becomes somebody else's words, not yours, and you can bring yourself to be merciless, as Bill will be. You consider each sentence as you read it. You turn it a thousand ways before letting it, grudgingly, from your grasp. During this process, you are moving sentences around, breaking up sentences, transposing words, bringing to the fore important points that are buried in internal paragraphs, using the correct word rather than the ballpark one you allowed yourself to put in before. You work in a white heat. Does Bill get it?

30. Revise again

When you're finished doing this out loud (rule of thumb: ten minutes per page if you're a wobbly writer), do it again silently. Here's how: you take another piece of paper and cover all but the first line of your printed copy. Take your hand off the cover sheet so you're not tempted just to glide it down the page of your writing. Your job is to look at the line exposed as the cover sheet is drawn down your writing and make sure it's ready to pass inspection before moving the paper down to expose the next line. And the next. And the next.

31. Run a perimeter

A good quick run for midshipmen is a "perimeter," just inside the fence around the Naval Academy. It's about 3.6 miles. I always recommend that after midshipmen have Billed their paper out loud and then silently, they run a perimeter. And then come back and Bill it one last time. You'll be surprised at how many more problems you'll catch. This is so because you're no longer in the heat of the moment with respect to your ideas and sentences: you can see them from the outside.

Sleep on it, read it when you're fresh. Suddenly you can see it the way Bill does, and there are a thousand things to fix.

III

Your Own Private Grammar Friday

A: Why Study Grammar?
1. Grammar is scary

In my class at the Naval Academy, we have Grammar Fridays: ten minutes on a specific topic to show people what the issue is and why they need to think about it. You can have your own Grammar Fridays, and they don't have to be just at the end of the week.

Grammar is scary for many people because it seems so abstract, so far from what we really do with language—at least if it's the grammar of the language we grew up learning. Frequently grammar is presented in class as something we have to master before we can even start writing, something that we do wrong. Instead, considering grammar is like going to a golf pro for lessons. Nobody says you can't play golf without the lessons. It's just that the lessons make you better. For some reason people haven't been encouraged to see grammar as a way to improve their game. Nobody is telling you you have to be able to analyze the atomic structure of water before you can go to the water fountain. But there are circumstances where knowing the structure of water can be useful. We express abstractions like grammar points or atomic structure because doing so has a point: they're more general than the specific cases. If we don't have problems with the specific cases, we don't need the general. The purpose of talking about the general is to clarify problems with particulars. But the general has no point by itself, only as a means to understanding the particulars. The teacher will do well to make sure people understand what the point is.

2. What is grammar?

When you write for Bill you're juggling many balls at the same time: you're thinking about the size hole you have to fill, you're thinking about the way you're saying it, you're trying to get clear yourself about your main points, you're trying to put the words together in the ways that written language requires (sentences), you're trying to link ideas using the squiggles we use (punctuation), and you're trying to choose the precise word with the right set of meanings to hit the right tone. Because of fact that you have to keep many balls in the air at the same time while remaining conscious of all levels of problem from the largest (does this fill the right hole and is it a plausible fill?) to the smallest (which of two words do I need here?), writing is like any other situation in life where you have to use words. When you're asking someone for a date you have to be able to ask the question itself, you have to get the right wording, and you have to get the right intonation to sound interested and available but not desperate. All that in perhaps a sentence or two.

Grammar is the codification of mid-level considerations because those are the ones that can be codified most easily. There's no grammar book that will help you decide whether what you're saying is important enough to say; there's no grammar book that will help you decide whether you've used just the right word for your purposes. Grammar narrowly understood (in the area where there are rules) is about only what's in the middle. There's no equivalent of grammar exercises for the largest considerations, like "Is this an important enough issue to consider?" There's no equivalent of grammar exercises for things like "do I want this precise word, or this one?"

Things at the ends, the largest and the smallest considerations you have to keep in mind when you write, are too specific to be codified, so they aren't. Because grammar can be taught, that's what *is* taught. Grammar is the stuff in the middle. That doesn't mean it answers all of questions.

3. Prescriptive and descriptive grammar

Nowadays the position is popular in academic circles that grammar should not be prescriptive, telling people what to do, but descriptive, saying how people actually use language. Perhaps this feels liberating: throw off the shackles. But following the rules isn't constraining. It's the only way you can hope to get through to Bill, because he knows the same rules. Rules are what you have in common. You need them to communicate.

Englishmen and -women living in India in the nineteenth century who learned "kitchen Urdu" could say rudimentary repetitive things to the cook. Those who learned better Urdu could have complex discussions about real topics with local intellectuals. There are levels of mastery of a language, and hence limitations on what you can say depending on how many of the rules you've mastered. The same is true of any language, even the one we grew up speaking.

The prescriptive grammar camp thinks that grammar consists of rules that have to be upheld. The descriptive grammar camp thinks that all rules do is track the changes make to the way we collectively use language. Extreme members of the descriptive grammar camp hold that people can't make mistakes in language.

Of course you can make mistakes in language, just the way you can tell a joke that falls flat. Still, if you can identify the beaten path and think you can navigate the area off it, by all means give it a try. You could even show up in a T-shirt at a board meeting if you had a good enough reason or explanatory story or enough leverage. If you're a junior member who's on thin ice for other reasons, however, and your reason is merely that you felt like it that day, it's not a good idea. Go with the default: wear a suit. Everything depends on context. And that in turn means, you have to assess the situation accurately, know how it's going to play to Bill.

Nowadays the people with power seem to think they don't have to do it right. The critics pointing out they're not doing it right have only the power to criticize, so grammar "gotchas" seem weak and annoying to people in the driver's seat. If you have your dignity as a functioning adult to defend, you're likely to be defensive if somebody corrects you when you make mistakes. You're just a critic, and I'm an officer in the U.S. Navy! I'm Vice President of General Motors!

Of course you are. If you remember Bill, the defensiveness born of the sense that somebody is trying to rap your knuckles goes away too. This isn't you against the person correcting you. This is you trying to get through to your buddy Bill. If you didn't make it through to him, or caused him trouble, that's something you should want to hear about.

Sometimes the grammar gotchas go on for so long about how disgusted they are that reasonable people get disgusted with the grammar gotchas. Oh no! You broke rule #527! The reasonable people point out that such rules change all the time. If you read the poems of Emily Dickinson, for example, you'll see a frequent use of the apostrophe for the possessive form of "its": his, hers, it's. So it's not as if there's any absolute reason why we should make the distinction between "it's" and "its."

Someone thinking like Bill, who can ignore the grammar gotchas, would say, that was then and this is now. We have that distinction now, so using one rather than the other confuses people who know what the distinction is.

It's more comfortable to stay in your own head and insist the problem isn't you, it's everybody else. To the plebe locked inside his or her own head, what's on the paper looks fine. It's only when I Bill it back to them and they have to endure what Bill endures that the light bulb goes on.

"Oh," they say. Which I translate, perhaps giving in to my fantasy, as: "I get it. This paper is not something whose life ends when it exits from my printer back in Bancroft Hall [the midshipmen dormitory]. This is something whose life is only starting. And who knows what byways it will go down, who will read it?"

So writing for Bill means getting over your annoyance at the grammar gotchas. But it would also be nice if the grammar gotchas stopped acting as if the sky falls every time someone makes the error of (say) a comma splice (see below). It usually takes more than that to have Bill stop running with you. If you're very important, people will never stop running with you. But you should realize what they're thinking and saying when you're not around.

If you're applying for a job, it may not take much more than a comma splice for your application to be tossed out the window. The boss may not be able to label it a "comma splice," but s/he'll be puzzled. What do these two things have to do with each other? If this person can't be clear in a job application, when *can* s/he be clear?

Bill is like the customer: he's always right. He comes to your writing seeking to understand. If you give him mis-cues, he won't. You aren't justified in having hurt feelings if he leaves your store. "Come back, Bill!" you want to call. "You could see what my main point was!" Bill is long gone. There are other stores, and if need be, he'll do without.

Grammar Friday
4. In the pool

One day in the Naval Academy pool, a retired Army officer who swims regularly was shaking his head about the decline of the English language. "What's happened to 'shall'?," he asked. "Nowadays everything is 'will.'" He evidently expected me, as an English professor, to sympathize.

I felt embarrassed that I didn't see much difference myself. I didn't dare show myself one of those "anything goes" sorts by saying that I thought "shall" had pretty much had its day, like "should" in the following sentence: "I shouldn't do that if I were you." We'd all say "would." Of course, we do preserve "shall" for commands, that we say with a booming voice to show how archaic we know they are: "It shall be done!"

But one (wo)man's meat is another's poison: I recently read a grammar gotcha who claimed some sympathy for the shall/will distinction, but none at all for the who/whom distinction. He said that "who" had definitively won out over "whom." The who/whom distinction, however, makes sense to me, at least under certain circumstances. Sometimes it seems necessary, and sometimes it seems silly.

I'd say, do it when necessary and when it's silly, don't. Usually we let the "m" drop: "Who'd you get that from?" But sometimes the fact that the who-form is the object of something, whether preposition or verb, needs to be acknowledged. As in: "The man from whom I learned French." We'd think it funny to read: "The man from who I learned French." Most of the time, we'd avoid the issue by saying, "The man who taught me French," or more informally, "The man I learned French from." Avoiding difficulties is as much a skill in writing as doing correctly what you do.

Sometimes the distinction between "who" and "whom" clarifies an important structural distinction. Is the person the actor or the acted upon? The more general problem of not understanding whether the pronoun is the do-er or the done-to produces the problems many writers (and speakers) have with "I" and "me" or with "he" and "him." They don't know which one to use, so they stop dead, and don't know how to figure it out.

People don't get this wrong all the time, only sometimes. They'd never say, "Ben came to the gym with I." It has to be "me" because "me" is so clearly the object of the preposition "with." They'd always say, "Give me a chance," never "Give I a chance." Yet Bill Clinton heard from the grammar gotchas when he said, "Give Al Gore and I a chance." This is wrong to my ear too. I register the "give" and know that what has to follow is an indirect object. "Chance" is the direct object. I'm primed for the indirect object of "me" so I need it. But I know Bill Clinton would never say, "give I a chance." In his ear, "Al Gore and I" had a certain unity, and he was inserting the whole phrase into the longer sentence.

That's just the argument that the linguist Stephen Pinker makes, in a book called *The Language Instinct*, in considering just this example. He's one of those people who claim that people don't make mistakes in language. Pinker thinks that speaking for people is like building nests for birds: for both, the activity is something they do naturally.

Pinker's theories seem silly with languages we've set out to learn—such as, say, French or German. If an individual can't make mistakes in language, why do we allow ourselves to be corrected by the French or German teacher?

Oh, Pinker might say. I mean that no *native speaker* of a language can make mistakes. But how do we define "native speaker"? My daughter has been diagnosed with Asperger's Syndrome, a mild form of autism. I taught her to speak English, her native language. We played with rubber duckies on the floor: "The duck is *in* the box. The duck is *in front of* the box." "This duck is *bigger than* the other duck." Was I wrong to correct her when she said "next to" when she should have been saying "in front of"? Am I wrong to correct my older son, apparently normal but not yet three, when he says "me and Mommy are going to the store"? "Mommy and *I*," I say. I need to hear a word that functions as a subject, not an object. Mommy and *I* are going to the store; Daddy drove Mommy and *me*.

Oh, Pinker will say. I mean, *non-disabled adult native speakers*. How about non-disabled adult native speakers *who don't pay attention to the way language is used*? Am I supposed to smile when one of my students writes that Shakespeare's sonnet "instills immortality on the words of his poem" (instills *on*?) or informs Bill that an "idea is started" (you can start *thinking* about an idea but we don't say, "start an idea"), or says that someone has "become numb to the sounds" (mixing a feeling metaphor with an aural one)? Or, moving past the merely annoying into deal-breaker territory, when they put what is clearly the main idea of their paper in the middle as an aside, buried in a paragraph about something else? Or when the last paragraph is by far the clearest exposition of the paper's point so that Bill has had to flail for three pages hoping to be rescued? Bill does not smile, and neither do I.

Perhaps advocates of descriptive grammar mean only is that God doesn't care whether we say "who" or "whom." Of course not. This isn't about God, it's about Bill. If the sentence is set up so that Bill needs to hear something in the objective or accusative case (with *me*) to understand that it's the done-to rather than the do-er, then you need to be able to put it in that case. It may be it's clear enough from the sentence who's the doer and who's the done-to, so you can fudge and use "who" rather than "whom."

Descriptive grammar people seem to be saying I shouldn't have to think when I speak or write. We sometimes have to think when we speak other languages. Why not in rocky places of English? There are times in my life when I have to pick my words very, very carefully, even—or especially—when I'm talking English, and times when I can just run on. Each of us has to know which is which and act accordingly.

5. *To willfully split*

My swimming pool buddy was also perturbed about the fact that it seemed acceptable nowadays "to willfully split" (as he said, smiling) an infinitive. What did I think?

I think whether or not it's acceptable is determined, as always, by how you want Bill to react. Splitting an infinitive breaks up things that normally are written together (to do, to be, to eat, to drink). Do you want to emphasize, by the disruption, the word that's being shoved in the center of the infinitive? Split away. "To boldly go where no man has gone before" emphasizes "boldly." But be aware of what the effect of doing that is. If that's not the effect you want, don't do it.

The most bitter grammar battles are fought over the smallest issues because they are the ones in the gray area, the ones we don't need commonality about. We can get up a head of steam to argue some point precisely because it's undecided, which almost invariably means, it depends on circumstances. So ask your Bill and be done with it. Nobody argues that we should accept "I are" for "I am," and the number of people is dwindling who argue that we should accept "I be good" to show cultural sensitivity. Instead we go on about shall/will, who/whom, or whether it's allowable to split the infinitive. The fact that those are all we have to argue about indicates that we're in agreement on all the rest.

In the same way that some people think they've proven something profound when they insist that there's no wrong or right in writing (they haven't), they think they've made a major point by noting that language is made of conventions with no absolute value. To which Bill says, "Roger that" (correct; I read you). Sure, it's a convention to capitalize the pronoun "I" when we're speaking about ourselves. It's a convention to put apostrophes in to indicate missing letters. It's a convention to start a new sentence with a capital letter (in British English, a majuscule). For that matter, it's a convention to divide groups of words into what we call sentences and put a little dot after them, like this.

If we really believe that not only the apostrophe in "it's" but all conventions can be thrown out the window, we don't have any way of getting through to Bill.

B: Bill's Brand of Grammar
1. The topic

Part of writing is figuring out what to say. That means, deciding what to put in and what not to put in. What doesn't make it to the page is as much a part of writing as what does. Wobbly writers have too narrow a view of writing when they equate writing with correcting a few commas. Writing involves much more fundamental issues, like: where to start?

Starting something is typically very difficult for wobbly writers, because they see the words on the page, or the screen, as the end whereas in fact they're on the means. The lack of words on the screen causes them to freeze. No words seem any better than any other. Where to start?

But if they look beyond the words to the purpose of the writing, the words begin to flow. You're not counting drops any more, you're trying to fill up the glass. If you look down at the hole, it seems very deep. What to do? Yet if you look beyond the hole to the other edge you can see the hole as merely something to be filled, and get started filling it.

You go into the hat store and say, "I need a hat." That's already more precise than saying, "I sense the vague desire for something, but I can't tell you what." It's also clearly not the same thing as other things you might have said, such as "I need a fishing pole." So you've got some sense of the hole. You may have an even clearer sense of the hole, but the salesperson doesn't. So s/he asks. (You've noted I like "s/he"—an invented non-word I find very useful and not unduly offensive, but too much of it gets clunky, so let's say both the salesman and customer are male.) "What kind of hat?" he says. "I don't know," you say, not being wise to the ways of the hat world.

The salesman begins to help you narrow down the purpose: he's thinking like Bill. "What do you need it for, sir?" he asks.

"Well," you say. "I have to go to a picnic."

Picnic means summer. The salesman knows that nowadays the only hats men wear to picnics in the summer are somehow "retro" hats. Unless, that is, what you had in mind is a ballcap, which you probably have several of already. And it's highly unlikely that you'd go into a proper hat store to get a ballcap. Not impossible: if you're from another country, say, or very young, or simply unaware of who sells what, you might well do this, and it might turn out that the salesman's presuppositions are wrong.

But let's assume you know that you don't need a hat store to buy a ball cap. So when you say a picnic, the salesman assumes you mean, a formal, rather retro picnic.

He might say: "Do you want a boater?"

"A what?" you ask. "No, I'm not going boating. I'm going to a picnic. You know, food on the grass. That sort of thing."

The salesman is patient. "A boater is a kind of hat. Straw, with a flat brim and top, and with a band around it."

"Oh," you say. "Is that what it's called? Yes, that's exactly what I need. Gatsbyish."

"What color ribbon?" the salesman asks.

"What colors do you have?" you ask. It's a legitimate question, even for someone skilled in the way of boater hats. Here the salesman is falling down on the job.

"One is alternating black and red," he says. "And we have this new color, green."

"I don't know," you say. "I'll have to see them."

The hole you're filling has still not been completely defined. Now he needs to know what your size is. This is a skilled men's hat salesman, and he barely glances at your head before disappearing and coming back a moment later with two hats in the same size that miraculously to you, turns out to be exactly the right one, one with red/black and the other green. You try on the green, then the other, then the green again. "This is it," you say. You pay and walk out happy, the hat in its bag, as you wouldn't be caught dead in the street in it before your picnic.

The next time, should there ever be a next time, you'd know to say, "Good morning, I'd like a boater in size 7 7/8 please. What colors of ribbon do you have?" Here the salesman has been your Bill, helping you to define the way you express what you need to express. The trick about writing for Bill is that you have to be your own salesman, your own Bill. You have to define your situation by yourself.

2. Setting things up

Written or verbal use of language can go wrong if you are unaware of the size of the hole you are filling. This almost inevitably means, you've failed to identify your Bill. Let's look at an example.

Since several people drowned in the Naval Academy pools in the 1990s, there have been signs that scream "No Swimming Without Lifeguard." At the Naval Academy this is understood as an order, not merely a suggestion. The swimming time during the noontime hours is from 11:45 to 1:45. Occasionally, sometimes often, over the years I've been swimming, the lifeguard has been late, or failed to show up at all. The lifeguards are usually young women provided by a lifeguard service, one whose contract changes as often as the cleaning companies in the academic buildings, every year or two. Perhaps they don't understand the importance of punctuality at the Naval Academy, where plebes are screamed at to "find your sense of urgency!" Or the fact that at 11:45 there will be as many as a dozen people in bathing suits—midshipmen, officers, and professors—lined up watching the clock. Few things are more infuriating than having a dozen suited-up people pressed for time, many of whom have hustled to be there early to get lanes, wait for someone who saunters in 15 minutes late with no apology. (Apologies in a social situation, incidentally, are a way of acknowledging the default and trying to negotiate the distance between what you have and what Bill expects.)

One day, the lifeguard was in fact late. I watched the clock, set artificial Rubicons that were twice crossed (if she isn't here in two minutes I'm putting my clothes back on and leaving), commiserated with the other waiting would-be swimmers, and dove in disgustedly when finally she did drift in.

Thus the next time, the particular one in question, as I pushed open the doors at 11:44 and 55 seconds, I was delighted to see the guard, another one, taking the last step to her chair. At 11:44 and 58 seconds she was sitting in it, ready for business.

How to tell Bill this story? Here's what won't work:

"The lifeguard was in her chair at 11:44 and 58 seconds today."

Bill doesn't know how this relates to the expected, so he has no idea how to react. Two seconds as opposed to two minutes? Why is this worthy of comment? Is the lifeguard not supposed to be there then? Bill may have a hunch that the witching hour is 11:45 because this is so close to a round-number time, here a quarter of an hour, but it isn't clear. 12 sharp is a more probable witching hour, so it looks as if she's there 15 minutes early—though this leaves in question why the seconds are being calibrated.

Slightly more conscious of Bill is: "The lifeguard was in her chair two seconds early today."

But still we don't know how important this is, or why we should be interested. Perhaps Bill can figure out that the only reason we should be interested is if at some point she wasn't two seconds early, but we don't know what this is, or whether she's usually 5 seconds early, 5 seconds late, or a no-show.

So we have to set it up so the thing we want to emphasize comes out: that she was, instead of being 15 minutes late, absolutely punctual, so punctual that save for a second or two, her bottom was contacting the chair at the appointed time, as punctual as a Naval Academy midshipman with a "sense of urgency."

What we should tell Bill, then, is something like this: "Instead of being unbelievably late like the last time—when swimmers who had hustled to be right to the minute of 11:45 cooled their heels and watched the seconds change on the digital clock—today the life guard, perhaps the recipient of harsh words about her performance the last time, was lowering her bottom into the chair exactly as the numbers changed to 11:45, the beginning of the session, or with a second or two to spare."

Not setting it up properly is like handing Bill a map of the world every time you want to talk about one country, or focusing on a city when your real subject is the country. Movies "set up" shots in the same way: first the Eiffel Tower, where the purpose is not to get us to think of the Centennial Exhibit that produced it, or the engineer Eiffel who designed it, or the now long-gone animosity of the Parisians to this girdered giant looming over their generally low-lying city, but instead merely to signal "Paris." The next shot is then of the outside of a Paris café, and the following an inside room where two men are plotting the destruction of the West, two lovers meeting clandestinely, or two twenty-somethings oh-so-chicly bemoaning their boredom. And then the story begins. Or rather, the story has already begun.

3. Topic sentence and openers

Not all pieces of writing have a topic sentence. In some cases we need to look at two continuous sentences to get a sense of the topic. In some cases we have, instead of a topic sentence, what I call a "hot spot": you need a whole passage to see where the paper is going. Sometimes the situation provides the context so completely that the hole is already well defined and the writing can just fill it. If the assignment is to write a paragraph about your home, you just write a paragraph about your home. Yet even here the topic should be clear to an outsider: someone picking up the piece of writing should know that it's a paragraph about your home.

Wobbly writers sometimes write openings that don't give enough information. They may tell Bill what the desired end result is, but give no reason to think this is plausible. It's just as frequent to have an opening—usually a first paragraph—that's too long and leaves Bill guessing about why he's being told what you tell him. The issue in both cases is not absolute length, but timing. Wobbly writers haven't learned to pace themselves: to give a short version of the course for openers and then run the course. Either they give too little or too much. You have to find the middle ground between too much and too little detail.

Many wobbly writers have to get themselves up to speed when they write. Bill neither needs nor wants to watch you get up to speed. He's ready to go right now, when he picks up your writing. He has other things to do. There's nothing wrong with writing these get-up-to-speed openers, but cut them off when you revise (you may have to re-work the opening at that point).

In your opening, give Bill the basic idea. In this run, we're going to take a loop around the lake. It's about 4 miles. There's a little bit in the middle where mothers walk baby-carriages but they drop off when you get to the woods. There's an uphill near the end. What do you say we sprint that? That makes an excellent opening. You haven't gone into details, just given Bill the big picture.

Openings are exercises in timing. We all have to learn how to do things in life that are appropriately timed: when to announce an engagement, when to break off a relationship, when to give the bad news, and when the good, and how much time we spend on each. Writing is no different.

Too narrow a focus on the "topic sentence" rather than the big-picture issue of timing isn't productive with wobbly writers. They immediately begin to ask for one-size-fits-all answers to "what do I do?" questions. Sir, should the topic sentence be at the beginning of the paragraph? Sure. Should it be at the end? Sure. Can it be the first sentence of the next sentence? Sure. If you understand the purpose of a topic sentence, or hot spot, you can decide yourself, based on whether or not the purpose is achieved. Instead of learning a rote answer to questions about a topic sentence, ask instead: "Does Bill understand what he needs to know when he needs to know it?" There has to be something on your mind. What is it? Answer that question and you can answer the question about where the topic sentence should be.

If the first paragraph takes up most of the first page of a three-page piece of writing, the topic sentence—which really means, the point at which Bill has a sense of the largest overview of the course he's going to run with you—can't be a third of the way through. Probably the paragraph is too long. Fix that first, then decide where it's appropriate to give Bill the map of the course, which is what the topic sentence or hot spot does. Still, getting this one thing right, important though it is (openings, like first impressions, count for a lot) is merely getting this one thing right. Even if you get the timing and placement correct, you can still misuse words to the point where Bill has no idea what your point is, or send the wrong message with punctuation, or can set up the beginning of a structure and fail to finish it. You have to keep all the balls in the air at the same time.

Example: lamps
Let's say your topic is telling Bill about your mother's lamps.

Your opening is this: "My mother has been collecting lamps since before I can remember. When I came into the world, I was already surrounded by lamps. In my room alone there were nine. I know because I counted them over and over, those times when I was sent to my room for misbehavior. It wasn't a good place to send me for punishment. It was far too interesting a place to be. The rest of the rooms of our house were comparably outfitted, from the stand-up 1930s lamp with the cone that threw a light up on the ceiling and the ring of smaller bulbs that had to be turned on 1-2-3, pip pip pip, to the lava lamp left over from a hippie phase my mother was far too old to have gone through, to the *moderne* sprays of tiny lights at the ends of dandelions of Lucite rods that at some point were undoubtedly the last word in chic."

That's a pretty good first paragraph, or at least I think so. I made it up for purposes of illustration (I wasn't born surrounded by lamps). The point here is, don't let the leash out too far or kept it too short. If you let the leash out too long, you sabotage this opening. It's sabotaged if, for example, you go through the nine lamps in your bedroom in one by one detail (we don't have the overview yet). Or go into the history of the lava lamp, and all the other places you'd ever seen one. Or give an exhaustive description of lying on your back mesmerized by the changing blobs of the melting "lava" as it bubbles slowly inside—all this in the first paragraph.

No rule can explain why these are too much for an opener, and should come later, if at all, when you've settled down to a sustainable pace. They just are, the way you hand a bouquet of flowers to someone you're trying to impress and say, merely: "I thought you might like these" or "I remembered you like purple": you don't explain that you had larkspurs by your house when you were small—at least not then, not there—or that you got them in the supermarket but you hope she'll think you went to a florist, or that you looked at another bouquet but decided this was all you could afford. That's too much information. Instead, you just give them. If the recipient of your flowers seems interested, you might add the other information later. But maybe not.

Similarly, no book can indicate the point at which we say once too often that we're sorry, or upset. But the existence of books about grammar and composition and the non-existence of books about what we'd have to give up and call "Life" makes people think that writing is somehow different. It isn't.

The problem with too much detail is that it's inconsistent with the level of detail elsewhere in the same passage. If Bill expects the details at a certain speed, he's not upset at getting them at that speed.

4. Maintaining a consistent speed

Here's the second paragraph of my novel *Twilley*, with the opening modified. It's a lot of detail, but because Bill isn't expecting something different, he's probably not too upset.

> The rain flows over the edge of the grating in the cement at his feet, covering every bar of metal near that edge with a sheath of fuzzy thick clearness, the liquid form of the ice that occasionally in the winter coats all the twigs with smooth vests of glass. The effect is to further obscure the right-angle neatness of this so-carefully constructed grid and to change the surface beneath from something akin to several layers of gray felt to a hopelessly soggy mess, half puddles and slushy slime which, as the rain pocks it directly or falls from the metal in great ragged sheets, sends shooting upward in reaction unevenly-shaped drops and gouts of the muddy water which splatter the pieces of trash that are becoming more and more deeply imbedded in the slush, coloring them a uniform gray-brown so like the surrounding background that soon it will make no difference to anyone that they are not aligned with the precision they might be.

Bill probably wouldn't object that this is taking too much time on a sewer grating, since the first paragraph has been about the cigarettes beneath the grating. And the rest of the book continues at this speed. It takes the unnamed "he" more than 200 pages to walk down a city street and go through a department store, so buffeted is he by a swirl of close details. Bill notes the details and is supposed to ask, Why? It turns out the character's wife has left him and he's still in shock, so he's slipped the grooves that carry most of us forward in the daily round; the world has turned into something that's too full of little pieces with no coherence tying them together.

When Proust published the first volume of his vast work, that was initially translated into English as *Remembrance of Things Past* (later as *In Search of Lost Time*), critics objected that it took scores of pages for the protagonist Marcel to fall asleep. What would the rest of the book be? Thousands of pages later, they found out. This kind of deliberate departure from the normally expected speed is more possible in fiction than in works with more defined circumstances—which is the more fundamental difference between fiction and non-fiction, not that one is "true" and the other not.

But of course, if you're a Bill who simply won't read a book where it takes the protagonist dozens of pages to fall asleep, as in Proust, or 200 pages to find the bathroom (that's what the protagonist of *Twilley* is doing in the department store), you don't have to. Bill isn't out to change your personality or your taste, just trying to keep you from feeling betrayed. If the work gives no signs of changing speeds without explanation, you can't feel betrayed. It's not badly written; you just don't like it. There's a difference. Put that book down and pick up another one.

For that matter, some people don't like fiction at all. They'd much rather have a good book of military history. They're Bill's kind of guys and gals too. The length of the leash in a book on military history is probably going to be the same length as the leash in another book on military history. The reader knows what to expect. And the leash is going to be pretty short. Part of what keeps the leash short is crisp sentences and paragraphs. Another is that it makes frequent evident contact with a world we know to be true, talking about names and dates, the common structure of the way we talk about the world. In a fiction work, to a greater degree, you're at the mercy of the author. You agree to allow the writer a longer leash. Instead of asking, Is this true? on the first page, you let the work give you information without questioning it until quite a way in. (I return in Part V below to the question of what makes fiction the kind of writing it is.)

5. Paragraphs

Paragraphing is the way we show in Western languages that we're breaking up ideas into groups and allowing mental breaths by the readers. Here as elsewhere, no rule book can tell you what that length is. It depends on how many ideas you have and how long you have to lay them out.

Paragraphing isn't like taking an extant piece of material and making cuts at regular intervals: you actually have to weave the cloth for the area you have in mind. You can have a big fluffy paragraph followed by a shorter denser one. The length of the paragraph on the page can vary; what shouldn't vary is the weight of the material in each paragraph.

Otherwise it looks to Bill as if the smaller points should be combined into one paragraph.

Paragraphing to show the beginning of new ideas helps, but it's a fairly blunt instrument. We don't have a way to use paragraphs to show that paragraph 5 is a development of paragraph 4, not on equal level with 2, 3, and 4. The philosopher Ludwig Wittgenstein was sufficiently bothered by the bluntness of the paragraphing tool that he organized his first masterpiece, the *Tractatus Logico-Philosophicus*, on a system of decimal numbering that showed more closely the relationships between sections than paragraphs can. 2.12 was the second observation that linked to 2.1, for example, and of equal importance with the first observation, 2.11.

This system hasn't been widely adopted. I've experimented with indenting paragraphs further or less far depending on whether they're main ideas or subsidiary to earlier paragraphs. But this hasn't caught on either. I have plebes draw arrows on the short, journalistic essays we analyze at the beginning of the year: what sentence hooks to what? What paragraph to what? This too is a form of Wittgenstein's numbering, an attempt to make up for the insufficiencies of the paragraph indentation as a way of transmitting information.

Still, as a single arrow in the writer's quiver, paragraphing is useful. To get them right, ask a version of the columnist Ann Landers' famous question for women contemplating divorce: Am I better off with him or without him? Do these ideas belong together more than they belong apart? There's no absolute answer to the question: it depends on what's going on in the rest of the paper.

What we typically do to supplement the deficiency of the paragraphing tool is use the paragraphs insofar as we can to indicate new ideas, and use words within the paragraph to show the precise relationship of this paragraph's ideas to earlier ideas. Let's say we're extolling the beauties of the Naval Academy and list three major examples: the well-kept lawns, the constantly-changing flowers in the garden plots, and the neatly dressed students that populate our campus. Yet if, at some point, we insert an explanation that the flower displays vary by season and personal taste of the gardeners (for a time we had one with a tropical flair, so that our resolutely mid-Atlantic campus was feathered with banana trees surrounded by tropical flowers), there's no way to use just paragraphs to show that this idea is an expansion of the second item in our initial list. In fact, we may avoid paragraphing altogether. If we can limit this information to a single sentence, we'll probably include it in the paragraph about the plantings. If we want to expand on it, we give it its own paragraph so it doesn't balloon the paragraph about the plantings past the size of the paragraphs about the other aesthetic high points. But we'll begin the paragraph with a tag that makes clear to Bill that it's expansion on the topic of plants. "*These plantings* vary seasonally" may do it, if we've just been talking about plantings, and it's clear to Bill what "these plantings" refers to.

6. Sentences

Sentences are like stones of which a wall is made. If the stones aren't correctly formed, the wall falls down. If you see the divisions of sentences and paragraphs as external things cutting off your flow, you won't understand them. They're not limits on flow, bottles to contain the liquid of words. Instead, they're like bubbles that harden as they hit the air: you blow them up from inside. You have to know when to stop blowing. If you think about Bill, you'll know when to stop blowing, just as you'll know when you need to be quiet in a social situation. You don't protest too much, or explain how the bouquet you did buy costs less than the one you didn't.

The essence of a sentence is a relationship between an actor and an action that isn't there merely as part of a larger relationship, but that stands alone. This is like saying that something that is going to be built into a wall of stones of various sizes has to be a stone. A stone is something with a rounded-off outer surface. The size can vary, but it can't have been brutally broken off, or else it doesn't look right and doesn't fit into the wall.

We call this unit of actor and acted-on a complete sentence.

The signs of a sentence are a capital letter (majuscule) at the beginning, and a period, or full stop, at the end. These aren't sufficient conditions, only necessary ones. These aren't what make something a sentence, only the sign that you're offering it as such. They give a package of words the "look" or finish of a sentence. If the packaging of something like a sentence doesn't make it one, it does raise the expectation in Bill that it be one.

If you arouse a certain set of expectations in Bill, you don't have to fulfill them, but you have to be aware that he has them. Crying "Fire" means there's a fire, or at least you think there is one. Crying "Wolf!" means there's a wolf. Remember what happened to the boy who cried "Wolf!" when there wasn't one: when, subsequently, there *was* one, no one came to his rescue. This is the reason you "have" to write in complete sentences. (Someone weary of grammar gotchas would say, "I don't *have* to do anything!" No, but there are consequences. Such as this: nobody comes when you really do have a wolf.)

The most common reason for contravening the expectations associated with sentences is that you're quoting someone else who said it. This is why it's all right for fiction writers who include dialogue to leave the dialogue in incomplete sentences. It's not my fault, that's just the way this particular person said it! If you're the particular person, you don't have that excuse.

Conversations frequently take place in one-word units which are not complete sentences, and only make sense when strung together.

"Why?"

"Because."

"Because what?"

"Just because."

They're not sentences, but in conversation the context provides the rest of the structure, and in written form they're okay because you're quoting. If you're not quoting, but laying one stone on top of another, the stones have to be able to support each other, which means each one has to have all its parts.

Something like this is not a complete sentence: "Because of the way you look." Of course we can say it, just as there can exist objects like broken stones: it's a complete misunderstanding of the role of grammar in the world to think that what the grammar books say somehow determines the raw material of the world. Perhaps it's the response to the question, "Why don't you like me?" Grammar books at their best generalize about the effects of certain signs on the page; they don't say you can't have other things. But the only place I can think of where it would be acceptable is as dialogue in a short story or novel.

Long and short sentences

Here's a complete sentence of a single word: "Repent!" We understand that this single word presents a self-subsistent relationship of actor and action. Someone, unspecified, is telling someone else, implied, to do something: repent. That's a complete relationship. Something like this, however, is not: "Running along the busy highway that leads out of Santa Monica by the sea—a strip of fast-food joints, chain oil-change shops, discount big-box stores surrounded by parking lots that become abstractions of fish backbones radiating out from eerie blue-white lights in the middle of the night, a few cars apparently unable to find their owners abandoned in random places of the grid." (My example.) There are a lot of words, but structurally speaking it's all hanging on "running"—which tells us what's being done, but not what's doing it.

So it's not a complete sentence, which means: it doesn't fulfill expectations, and there's no evident reason why it should be given a pass for not doing it (such as that a character is saying it). Every rule has an exception, but if there's no evidence this is a justified exception, the rule is what you go with: that's how it's gotten to be a rule.

This is a complete sentence: "But I don't think so." This is not a complete sentence: "Although I don't think so." In the first case, that's the end of the statement. In the second one, you're waiting for the other shoe to drop. Probably this is the way it would be completed: "Although I don't think so, I may be wrong."

A grammar book will frequently say things like, "Because of the way you look" is not a complete sentence because "because" is a subordinating conjunction, so what we have here is a subordinate clause. A subordinate clause isn't a complete sentence.

But the reason "Because of the way you look" isn't a complete sentence is that it starts with a word that requires something else to make it a self-subsistent package. When it's the spoken response to a question, logically speaking it's part of a larger whole. The situation is what produces the whole. Stripped from this situation, it has to be able to stand alone, not be dependent on the situation.

At the other end of the spectrum from "Repent!" are very long and complex sentences indeed. But understanding what sentences do allows us to say why even things as long as these are a single sentence and not more. An example of a long sentence is the first sentence of my novel *Twilley*. The structure is complex to the point where I thought it was a good idea simply to repeat words to hold things together. The structure of the sentence is this: "**Noun verb object** of A, B C, C-prime (related to C), D, explanation of qualities of D, personification of qualities of D."

Grammar Friday

The **grid** over the subway vent **obstructs** his *view of* the spongy *floor* below, *of* the crumpled candy *wrappers* and the <u>cigarettes</u> <u>smashed</u> nose-or or <u>flattened</u> like a reed made from the tall swaying grasses which turn golden in the sun and rustle and brush the rippling white hem of our lover's dress as if exchanging whispered secrets, **obstructs** his *view of* the paper CUPS WHOSE BELLIES HAVE BEEN KNOCKED OUT and WHICH now LIE [deflated, the air having escaped through the gaping wounds, flaps with jagged edges between which the interior stuffing whooshed at so rapid a rate that no amount of gasping from the hideously distended mouth on the other side could replace it.]

This long sentence is full of subordinate clauses. Though a tree can be nothing but a single trunk with very little else, most trees divide into sub-trunks, these into branches, and these into smaller branches. Some have two or even more main trunks. In the same way, sentences can be made of all sorts of parallel and offshoot trunks and branches, any or all of which can fail to be completed properly (twigs of a certain diameter have to relate correctly to other twigs of the same diameter, as well as to the part of the tree they grow off of). Sentences can be long because they have many main stems, or because they have numerous smallest stems.

Compound predicates or sentences

Because the main trunk of the tree in a sentence is the self-subsistent unit of an actor to an action, the second most important thing to talk about after the structure of that trunk is how many trunks it has and where they go in relationship to it. Some sentences have two parallel trunks. Saying they're joined by a coordinate conjunction is the way we say this: it's not the fact that it's a coordinate conjunction that makes them parallel, but the other way around. "I like apples but I love pears"—this sentence has two trunks. "I like apples, though they are associated with the fall from the Garden of Eden"—this sentence has a single trunk and a large branch off it.

Given that clauses can be of two types, those that make parallel trunks or those that make smaller-bore but not necessarily less numerous sub-branches, writing manuals sometimes tell writers to make sure they vary their sentence structures. I see this problem most when the sentence structures in question are those of small, runty trees, each one only a single trunk. I mark this on student papers as --- --- --- --- ---. I have yet to object to a student paper on the grounds that the sentences are uniformly compound-complex sentences, which is to say well-developed trees with parallel trunks at various places in their structures and lots of smaller ones to fill it out.

Wobbly writers sometimes make what in structural terms is a very basic mistake, namely failing to agree the subject with the verb.

Agreeing subject with verb is so fundamental, we might wonder how anyone can do this one wrong. Usually it happens because the writer has lost track of what the subject is and what the verb. "Each of us have to give to the relief effort." The writer senses that "us" is plural and agrees "have" with the plural "us" (which can't function as a subject, because it's in the objective case) rather than the real subject "each." (It should be: "Each of us *has* to give.")

Sometimes either singular or plural can be justified, it's just that one seems more recommended than the other. "The reason we do so many drills and the way we do them is what we ought to stress." I'd say this has a compound subject, with two parts, so "is" needs to be "are." That's just the way it reads, as if we start with two things, so that they require a plural verb. But it's not impossible the real point here is that it's a sentence with one subject ("what we ought to stress") that then branches out into a predicate in two parts, what we call predicate nouns ("reason" and "way"). To justify this reading, and hence the use of "is," however, we should probably turn the sentence around, beginning with "What we ought to stress." Here, that doesn't seem to be the sense the writer is aiming at, so Bill is confused by "is." Similarly if we say "Love and money are what I need," that would change to "What I need is love and money" if we flip the sentence to change the subject emphasis.

7. *Completing patterns*

When you write, you initiate patterns that establish things you must do, while at the same time leaving things that are up to you. Writing for Bill means understanding that some things later on in the sentence, paragraph, or paper are implied by what you've already written.

If you start a sentence with "on the one hand," there almost has to be an "on the other hand" a bit later, either in this sentence or shortly thereafter. If you start a sentence with "Notwithstanding X," there has to be a "Y" that is unaffected by X and that you offer to Bill later on. If you start a sentence with "Standing on the shores of Lake Geneva," the next word almost certainly has to be the being doing the standing: a name or pronoun. (This is a "Superman"; see below.) If you start a sentence with "Not only," there had better be a "but also" at an appropriate time.

Agreeing subject with verb is also an example of pattern completion: you have to keep in mind what your actor is. Frequently when we talk, we do forget the structures we've set up: being attentive to what we say can help us complete the structures. Yet people "know what we mean."

If we say orally, "The reason he was late is *because* he was sick," probably no one will object, or even notice. However, if the sentence appears in written form, it's more problematic because the early part of the structure is still right there on the page. The *reason* is because? No, the reason *is* X. It's there on the page, staring at us; it hasn't disappeared into thin air the way spoken words do.

Many things that would pass as minor ripples in conversation take on great importance on the page. "Even though I love you doesn't mean I'm going to defend you in court." We might say it, but it's painful on the page. The structure set up by "even though X" requires something that's a Y to the X. There's some possible variation as to what exactly X and Y is: the sentence can be "Even though I *love* you, I'm not going to *defend* you." Or it could be "Even though *I* love *you, you* don't love *me*." Or: "Even though I love you, he doesn't love her." Or: "Even though I love you, I can still love her too." So you get to choose what you're going to pick up in the rest of the sentence.

Somebody asks: "What's track and field?" The verbal answer could very well be, "Track and field is where you run and jump outside." But when it's on the page, Bill balks. Track and field is *where*? No, surely not. "Track and field *is* X." (The title is a collective, "track-and-field," so it requires a singular verb.)

Sometimes the mis-cues of structures that aren't successfully completed are so strong that even with the additional context of a verbal delivery, we don't "get" it. This works neither verbally nor in written form: "I'm as concerned about you as much as Sally."

A speaker would know what this means, but Bill, the reader, doesn't. I'm concerned as much about you as Sally is? Or: as I am about Sally? So Bill has to ask. If it's written, as it may be, Bill has no one to ask.

8. *Punctuation*

Punctuation is the mortar holding the stones together into the wall. But you decide on punctuation as the same time you're making all the other decisions: Are my arguments clear? Have I agreed subject with verb? Have I made a clear transition from one point to the next and/or correct paragraphing decisions? The only way we can keep all these things in the air at the same time is by focusing on our goal, and on Bill. That way each of the decisions necessitated by answering these questions becomes a part in a larger whole, not a daunting end in itself that is capable of stopping us cold.

Sometimes punctuation is more important than other times, but even leaving it out even when it's not so necessary puzzles Bill.

Perhaps influenced by time spent on the computer, midshipmen sometimes write dialogue like this on creative writing projects:

"how are you doing"

"what a ridiculous idea"

Bill would have to read the first as a monotone. He's not dumb, so he sees it has to be a question. But you're making him add the intonation that "?" gives. This is a case where you don't really need the punctuation, but leaving it out is puzzling because it looks as if you're making some kind of point you aren't. Sometimes Bill can't tell the sense of a written sentence from which punctuation has been omitted. Take this example:

what do you think I'm going to do kill you

This one stops Bill cold. Is it: "What do you think I'm going to do? Kill you?" Or is it: "What do you think I'm going to do? Kill you!" Probably the first, to be clear, needs an indication of a tone of sarcasm. There's no way to get this into punctuation, unless a combination of a "?" and "!" does so, as in: "What do you think I'm going to do? Kill you?!" This may indicate the suggestion is so ridiculous as to be silly. However even this might not do it; you might have to say, "he said in a disgusted tone" to make the meaning clear.

Each of the arrows in a writer's quiver has its limitations, which is why you have to be able to take out any one at any time. Paragraph indentation won't show you what idea hooks to what, so you have to say in words what the relationship is ("as another example"; "to return to the earlier point," "by the way"). Breaking things into sentences doesn't show you if they contain a lot of information or a little, only that they can stand alone, whatever the amount of information. We have no way to show disgust in punctuation, but we do have ways to show emphasis ("!") and questions ("?").

If you're saying this sentence above ("what do you think etc.") rather than writing it, you can add the "?" at the end with your voice, and your inhalation before starting it and perhaps facial gestures shows your audience it's a new thought, something that on the page has to be shown by a capital letter. In written form, we add the markings that help us get back to where you can be if you're actually saying it to someone. The Instant Message-like scrawls above become things like this: "How are you doing?" and "What a ridiculous idea!" or perhaps, "What a ri*dic*ulous idea!"

Clusters

Some punctuation marks cluster together as alternatives to each other, though the whole cluster may present alternatives to other ways of making your meaning clear. The most efficient way to learn how to use them is to learn the cluster, both as individuals and a whole. One such cluster is the progression of comma, colon, semi-colon, and period (full stop). This cluster of punctuation marks build a scale of pauses, from short to mid-length to longer. Confusion among these is due to not asking yourself, How long a pause do I want to make? This is related to the question: How self-sufficient are the things I want to hook together?

Commas give a brief pause for things you want to keep fairly close together. This can be individual words in a list, or ideas that form a progression. They're a tap on the brake. Semi-colons give a longer pause. They're like a blinking yellow light: you slow and proceed with caution. Typically you want a longer pause between bigger units, such as stand-alone clauses joined into a single sentence. Colons are blinking red lights: you stop and proceed with caution. They're like trampolines: they push you forward after your stop. Periods, or full stops, are just that: full stops, a red light. Breaks between paragraphs are longer red lights. The end of the paper is the longest red light there is.

But not all points can be made using punctuation: sometimes we simply have to go outside the punctuation cluster, make our point using words or paragraph divisions.

Commas

Commas give people trouble because in English there are very few rules regarding how to use them. Wobbly writers in English as a result are unsure what to do with a situation where their discretion and judgment play a role. Somebody needs to tell them that being unsure is not only okay but the way things are.

If you can differentiate between the cases where you need a comma and where it's up to you, you're home free. You put them in when you need them and simply decide for the rest based on the effect you want to have on Bill.

Because commas break up the flow, you don't want to do that between subject and verb, verb and object, or the elements of a structure that go together, unless there's a specific effect you're trying to get that's not the usual one.

For example: "The Taj Mahal, is India's most famous building." You don't want to split the subject from its verb here unless you're trying to show a speaker who's paused portentiously and too long after "Taj Mahal."

Probably this person said it this way (I'd have to add some words in addition to the punctuation):

"The Taj Ma*hal*," he said, opening his eyes wide to emphasize to the children, "is India's *most famous* building." He looked around the circle, looking fixedly under his beetle brows at each child, to make sure all were duly impressed. The children giggled.

Here's another example that is wrong unless a particular effect is being aimed at: "Neither John, nor Sally, is going to do it." The unit of meaning is "neither x nor y," so normally you don't want to break it up. It's short enough that you don't want Bill to pause. The only time you'd do this is if you're trying to imitate a speaker who's emphasizing—somehow the presupposition is that Sally is going to do it, and he wants to make very clear this isn't so.

This is a good example of the fundamental fact about grammar rules: they're not moral laws you get punished for contravening. Instead, they're generalizations about norms. You can always do something else than what the rule calls for, but it's going to have an effect other than the usual. If that's the effect you want, break the rule—the rule itself has no power to stop you. All it does is help you see what most people want in such cases under most circumstances.

At the beginning of Sonnet 55, Shakespeare writes: "Not marble, nor the gilded monuments/ Of princes, shall outlive this powerful rhyme." Here he starts with "not," to which "nor" seems like an afterthought, hence separated with a pause (comma). Even if he'd chosen to write "*neither* marble *nor* the gilded monuments" he could still have gotten away with a comma. The comma would have indicated a sort of measured thought process, a breath made possible by the fact that the second element is longer: The gilded monument of princes (and you emphasize the word "princes").

Using a comma where we ordinarily don't produces this sense of pause, or reflection: we're showing thought process. It's not wrong, it's just a specific effect that has to be clear to Bill. Usually we say, "he went to and fro." But it's not wrong to write: "He went to, and fro"—pausing with our voice to indicate that he stopped when he turned around. To make this clearer we might say: "he went to, and he went fro." This is almost funny because we rarely break apart these elements: we don't have an expression any more with just "fro," as in "he went fro." P.G. Wodehouse is particularly adept at using words that ought to exist but somehow don't, as when he speaks of a character that "while not disgruntled, he was not positively gruntled either."

Commas in lists

Most people know that commas are necessary to separate elements in a list. At least, that's the grammar-book way of expressing it. On Grammar Friday, Bill says it this way: if you want to show that things are separate but equivalent elements, you put brief pauses between them.

Very few people would write the following: I like apples oranges peaches and papayas.

There is already some pause built into having separate words, but to show that the apples, oranges, peaches and papayas are things of equal order, we put commas between them. If, instead of putting in commas, we write "A and B and C and D" we're indicating a degree of fatigue at so many things piled on.

If reading the sentence with the commas, Bill understands when he hits the word "and" that there's only one more item in the list, so some people put a comma after "peaches" and some don't. Either one works. This sort of "up to you" choice is resolved simply by making a decision. Magazines and publications have "style sheets" that make such calls.

We can't put a single comma between "I" and "like" in the sentence above because these are the two elements of the sentence that have to be kept most fundamentally together. A single comma breaks them apart: it stops us for a split-second, which is a split-second too much. Bill would be confused, because he's trying to hook them together. However, two pauses around an expression we interject, where we'd drop our voice, don't confuse Bill. They indicate that what's bracketed in commas is of secondary importance. The sentence just above that begins with "Two pauses" has such an interjection ("where we'd drop our voice"). Bill removes it mentally and can re-join the essential parts.

We can come up with a situation to justify practically anything that our fingers can write. It's possible to write the sentence with the fruit, above, without commas: we might do so to indicate someone in a hurry or out of breath. But if we're merely giving Bill the information about the narrator's likes, rather than information about the delivery, lack of commas confuses Bill. Aren't these elements of equal importance?

Co-ordinate and non-coordinate adjectives

Another instance where you decide whether or not to put in a comma based on what information you want to give Bill involves the difference between adjectives of the same level of importance, co-ordinate adjectives, and adjectives that we can order according to the importance of these qualities to the noun.

If we say: "She combed her long shining black hair," we do not put commas between the adjectives, the qualities of the hair. If we say: "I hit the squashy, scuffed ball," we do need commas. You're giving Bill specific information by including them. The difference is that in the case of the hair, the adjectives are not equal: some are more fundamentally part of the noun, here "hair," than others are. The hair is more fundamentally black than it is long. You always arrange non-coordinate adjectives in the order from least fundamental to most fundamental. There are no commas, because the adjectives aren't equal and you don't need to keep them apart. In the case of the ball, it's not more fundamentally scuffed than it is squashy: both are temporary conditions. If it's a *rubber* ball, however, that is more fundamental than either of these qualities, and that has to come closest in the sentence to "ball." So it would be a "squashy, scuffed rubber ball": no comma between "scuffed" and "rubber."

The way you can tell if the adjectives are coordinate or not is by asking, Can you switch the order around with no problem? Usually we wouldn't say, "She combed her black long hair." If we did, it would be to quote someone without a grasp of English. If we said "She combed her black, long, shining hair," it would be to indicate the order in which some perceiver notes the qualities: first as black, then as long, then as shining. If this is the effect you want to give Bill, then that's how you write it. In any case, if it's written like this, this is the effect it's going to have on Bill, so that had better be the effect you want it to have. Grammar as a writer-adult consists of accepting the consequences of your actions. You can do practically anything, even the things you're told are wrong, or that you shouldn't do. The only thing is, doing that will have consequences: you have to know what they are so you can make a decision: is that what you want to happen? For that matter, being a moral adult means accepting that human beings are capable of practically anything: the only question is, once we understand what the implications of that action are, both for ourselves and others, is that what we want to do? For most people the answer is, no.

The default of what you say or write to your host after being invited out to dinner is some variation on "Thank you so much for a lovely evening." Of course you need not say that. You can say instead, "This evening was a disaster." But you had better want the reaction you'll certainly get.

Here are two sentences that do need commas, and if you read them for Bill I'm sure you'll put the commas there. "Those who can do." "Those who can't teach."

With commas, these become: "Those who can, do." Of course the pendant to this is "Those who can't, teach."

Sometimes it's not so clear if you need a comma, such as here: "I'd advise against it. However you can do absolutely anything you want." My impulse is not to have a comma after "however" because the whole sentence is going to its dramatic high point in the word "absolutely"— you don't want to break the back of the momentum to that place. Besides, you've just broken up your ideas with a period. If you eliminate "absolutely," I'd be much more inclined to put in the comma.

Restrictive and non-restrictive appositives and clauses

One of the most misunderstood uses of commas is in the case of what the grammar books call restrictive and non-restrictive appositives (an appositive is a second noun that says the same as the first, such as "Bill the Goat, the Naval Academy mascot") and clauses. But if we understand the point above that a single comma breaks things apart and keeps them separate, we need not bother with the terminology: we'll do it right without the technical terms. If an idea is fundamental to another, you don't want to separate it with the pause of a comma. If it isn't, and you want to add it as an aside, you put a pause before and a pause after to get the same effect on the page as dropping your voice in conversation. The idea restricts the meaning of the first, rather than adding information: it's a "restrictive" appositive, or clause (has a subject/verb).

Here's a sentence I often read on my students' papers. "Gustave Flaubert's novel, *Madame Bovary*, is the story of ..." *Madame Bovary* is the appositive to "Gustave Flaubert's novel." Here the wobbly writer has ended the unit of meaning after "novel" and provided information that's the equivalent of dropping your voice. The title becomes secondary information not necessary to the most fundamental unit of meaning. Hence what the reader has told me is that Gustave Flaubert wrote a single novel, and its title is *Madame Bovary*. This isn't so: Flaubert wrote a number of novels. Later on in the semester I have to explain to them that they can't write the following: "John Keats's poem, 'Ode on a Grecian Urn,' is xxx," because that tells me that he wrote only one poem. That's untrue.

Are there ever any circumstances under which this information might be what they want to say? Sure. If that's the only poem by Keats we've considered, they're saying, if they put in commas, that *in the context of our course* this is the only Keats poem. Or perhaps it's the only one in the book. But in writing outside of that context, putting in commas gives misleading information.

Here's something my mother-in-law said to my three-year-old recently. He was proudly showing her his collection of cicada shells. "I'm not a Nana who likes bugs!" She didn't write this; she said it. So I have to decide how to transliterate it on the page. Is it possible to write it with a comma? "I'm not a Nana, who likes bugs!"

No. In fact, this is factually incorrect. With the comma, you end the unit of meaning. My mother-in-law has said she's not a Nana (grandmother). That's untrue. And the rest of the sentence has to read as a rhetorical question that we sometimes punctuate with an ! rather than with a ? because it's not really a question: who could be crazy enough to like bugs?! So no comma, because the unit of meaning is [a Nana who likes bugs]—of course it means, the kind of Nana who likes bugs. "A Nana who likes bugs" is just the kind of Nana she isn't. So you can't have a comma in the middle; you need those things to stick together. It's so clear we do, probably we wouldn't even be tempted to write this sentence with a comma. But other times we'd hesitate; wobbly writers would freeze.

If we say "the first man who crossed the street before the others won the prize" we're setting Bill up to wait for other men who crossed the street (this is "restrictive"). "Who crossed the street" isn't separated from "the first man," so Bill assumes it's part of the fundamental unit of meaning. If you separate it out with a pair of commas, it's unclear what sense you mean "the first man"—it's something that has to be defined, but at least it's not defined by men who crossed the street. Perhaps the first man standing in a line (queue). So: "The first man, who crossed the street to get to the store before the others, won the door prize." This is non-restrictive, and it has another meaning entirely.

"That" and "which"

The question, Is my clause restrictive or non-restrictive? is related to the question, Do I say "that" or "which"? We say, "This is the best idea that I've had in a long time!" (Possibly we just eliminate "that.") This has no comma, because the unit of meaning is [the best idea I've had in a long time]. It's restrictive. But it's never "which": we just don't say, "It's the best idea which I've had in a long time."

For non-restrictive, something set off by commas, we can use "that" or "which." There's some tendency on the part of grammar gotchas to gild the lily and insist that because we use "that" for non-restrictive, we should consistently use "which" for restrictive. But in fact we can use either, so this is just the kind of rule that gives grammar a bad name. (Note: there's no comma between "rule" and "that" because the unit of meaning is [kind of rule that gives etc.]) "The answer is something stupid that I can't remember." But you can write either "The answer is something stupid, that I can't remember, and don't want to anyway" or "The answer is something stupid, which I can't remember, and don't want to anyway." Bill doesn't care.

In the first, the restrictive, the unit of meaning is that it's [something you can't remember] and in the second the unit of meaning is that it's [something stupid, and p.s., you can't remember it]. Functionally speaking, these are likely to be the same: you'll have to ask Bill if you need to make a distinction here. If not, then either one is all right.

Sometimes we're told that commas are used to show missing words. "John read one book; Bob, another." This is probably not appreciably clearer than "John read one book, Bob another." This one's up to you.

But sometimes the comma is necessary. "John read one book Bob another." That doesn't cut it with Bill. You read it from Bill's perspective to see if you have to have one, whether it might be nice if you felt like it, or whether you need to leave it out.

Comma splices

This is a comma splice: "I went to the store, I bought a loaf of bread." A grammar gotcha will howl bloody murder at this: comma splice alert!

You can write this, but it suggests that these two actions are of equal importance and otherwise unrelated. But that seems odd to Bill, who typically assumes some connection here. Most likely, you went to the store in order to buy a loaf of bread. Or you went to the store to get milk, but they were out, so you bought a loaf of bread because you realized you needed that too. These two ideas aren't completely unrelated.

Putting together two or more unrelated ideas with commas indicates somebody who's not in a normal frame of mind, or who is acting mechanically. Thus: I got up this morning, I had my coffee, I got dressed, I took the train to work. The information you're giving Bill here is that the person is somewhat distanced from his or her actions, and that they are performed in a chain, one after the other, with little mental engagement. For someone who wants this effect, that would be just the way to write. Usually, however, we don't want to give this information. Your teacher, or your boss, probably doesn't see any reason why you could possibly want to give this information in a paper for class or work, so s/he concludes it's a mis-cue to Bill.

Semi-colons

If you need the next size pause up, the semi-colon, typically it's because what you want to construct has larger units. The bolt is bigger, so you reach for a bigger nut. Typically semi-colons hook together complete sentences; that's so because they're stronger (note the use of the semi-colon in this sentence). Don't use a nut that's too big for what you need. It won't fit.

If you link two complete meaning units with a semi-colon, which is a longer pause than a mere comma, you acknowledge at least the fact that they're whole ideas. The information that doing this gives Bill is that the ideas are somewhat related, but not tightly. So sometimes this is just what you want to use; sometimes it isn't. It would still seem odd to say, "I went to the store; I bought a loaf of bread." This is still in the world of the disengaged, shell-shocked person who does first one thing, then the next, then the next, then the next.

Some wobbly writers don't know the difference between the first level of pause, indicated by a comma, and the next level, indicated by a semi-colon. Such writers might well put semi-colons between the kinds of fruit in the comma example above. But we only need the lowest level of division between the kinds of fruit, so we use commas rather than semi-colons.

What if you have a list of elements that themselves have commas in them? Won't it be confusing if your separation between the main elements of the list is also the lowest level of separation, more commas? Yes. And that's occurred to people. The result is that we allow what I call battlefield promotions of commas separating the major elements of the list into semi-colons. Consider, for example, the following: New York, New York, Albany, New York, Athens, Greece, Athens, Georgia. Things fall into place when we write this list as New York, New York; Albany, New York; Athens, Greece; Athens, Georgia. This is an attempt to rectify the bluntness of an instrument, here the comma, in the same way that Wittgenstein tried to rectify the bluntness of the instrument of paragraphing by introducing numbers to show more precise relationships between ideas than mere indentation allows. But it also proves the point that semi-colons provide a more robust pause than commas; use semi-colons only when that's what you need.

Colons

A colon is most typically a trampoline, as in this sentence, here: it stops you, you bounce, then go forward. It functions to show that what follows is an explanation of the part before the bounce.

People most typically use colons before lists: "There are three things I love about you: X, Y and Z." But you can use them any time you want to say "stand by, I'm going to explain or complete what I just said."

Hyphens

If you write a long list of words coming before the noun they collectively modify, you know all these words modify the noun at the end, because you know you have in mind. Bill doesn't. So in order to make clear to Bill that these words connect to each other to make a package that then connects to the noun he has yet to see, you join them with hyphens. Or at least you do this if you can read them the way Bill does and decide that the sentence is confusing without them. Not all these words will require commas anyway. If some of the words end in "ly" Bill realizes they're adverbs, which can modify adjectives, but can't modify nouns—so he's not tempted to say that they are going to modify the noun coming at the end of all this. And sometimes it's just clear: no one can give a rule that works 100%, so keep the hyphen possibility in mind without demanding a hard-and-fast rule (note the use of hyphens here). Of course, there are other uses for hyphens too, such as in numbers like "twenty-one"—you do it from twenty-one to ninety-nine and every time these recur, and to break words at the end of the printed line, though computers have taken over this usage for us, or made it unnecessary. But this one of extended adjective phrases (as we call these clusters before nouns) is the one that bears some discussion.

Here's an example of using hyphens to hook words together into a larger whole so Bill isn't confused: "The Naval Academy is a male-dominated society." If you write it without the hyphen, Bill thinks for a micro-second that you're saying it's a male society. It may be that too, but "male" isn't the same as "male-dominated": if 99 women do with one man says, the society is male-dominated but not, primarily, male. Another example: "This is a half-baked idea." It's not half an idea, but half baked. (If these clusters come after the noun Bill already knows what they modify, so you don't have to hook them together, as in the previous sentence: "half baked," not "half-baked," because after the noun. Similarly, we speak of a "two-year-old boy" but say, "my boy is two years old.") But note: "A badly thought-out plan"—Bill can tell that "badly," because it's so clearly an adverb, doesn't hook to any noun, but to the thinking out, so you don't need a hyphen. Adverbs that don't end in "ly" and aren't clearly adverbs ("well" is clearly an adverb even though it doesn't end in "ly" because it's so commonly used) might benefit from hyphens when used as parts of extended adjective phrases before nouns. If you think you need one, put it in; nobody will slap your wrist. Such as: "he's a fast-thinking but well-mannered young man." I'd put in the first comma, and am inclined to add the second one too, though it's not wrong to leave out the second.

9. Conjunctions

Give Bill the most precise logical connections between ideas that you possibly can. Explain to him what the relationship between going to the store and buying the bread is. Thus you probably want to avoid what are called "run-on" sentences, in which a series of events is hooked together with many instances of "and." You want to make levels of organization clear for Bill: tell him the biggest overview, the next biggest and so on, so he knows where a bit of information you're giving him fits into the structure. Otherwise it's just a list. That's a principle of organizing your writing into paragraphs and whole papers too.

Subordinating conjunctions imply very precise logical relationships between ideas by establishing a hierarchy. That's what the "subordinating" part means: you see what outranks what. That's useful when you're getting an overview, and helps avoid the effect of 1 + 1 + 1 + 1, which typically is difficult to follow for very long.

Subordinating conjunctions are things like this: *Although* I did X. *Because* of Y. *Even though* Z. You make clear the logical connections. But that means, you have to understand the connections yourself. Did he go to the store in order to get bread? Or just to go for a walk? For this reason, wobbly writers and children would much rather use co-ordinating conjunctions, usually a series of "and" or "but."

You can also make logical connections clear by ordering information under nouns, usually by relative pronouns: "The first man, who crossed the street before the others, won the door prize." This hooks the information that he crossed the street to the man with "who" so we know he's the one who crossed the street.

10. Word order

Words come to Bill in a line. He makes sense (or not) out of the words you feed him, in the order you feed him. Words that in the writer's mind clearly hook to one thing may seem to Bill to hook to another based on what's on the page. Sometimes this causes problems.

You might write: "I only tell you the truth."

Did you mean I only *tell* you the truth, I don't show it to you? Probably not, though that's what Bill infers. Bill always puts the things together that are closest to each other and that can be put together. So does it mean, I tell only you the truth? Or: I tell you only the truth? Bill can't say.

Consider this pair: "I'm extremely sorry to be the bearer of bad news." "I'm sorry to be the bearer of extremely bad news." These are not the same thing.

Word order conveys information in many ways. We hook qualities to nearby nouns just because we're being fed the sentence in a linear fashion. Here's an example I like: "The Venus de Milo was made by an unknown sculptor with no arms." Bill laughs because it seems you're saying it's the sculptor who has no arms.

Reference (again)

When we use pronouns, we have to be aware that Bill will assume they hook (or refer) to the closest plausible noun that precedes the pronoun, which may not be what we want to hook to at all. "I met the President and then went out to dinner with my brother. He smiled a lot." Was it the President or the brother who smiled? Either one would work, but because "brother" is closer in the sentence to "who smiled" and we assume the writer spent more time with the brother, it makes sense to think the brother was the one in the good mood. But we're not absolutely sure. Saying that "the President smiled a lot" is more natural than saying your brother did. You'd probably know why your brother was smiling, and tell Bill; you probably wouldn't know why the President was smiling, and leave it at what you saw.

Wobbly writers are fond of starting sentences with "this" or "it" without Bill having any idea what "this" or "it" is. The writer knows, but not Bill. [We all do it occasionally: my first version of the previous sentence was: "It's clear to the writer, but not to Bill." What is "it"?]

If I say, "Mark gave it to John and then he gave it to Sally," Bill doesn't know whether it's Mark or John who gave "it" to Sally. When you revise your writing, be on the lookout for "this" and "it", and be sure that Bill understands which "he" or "she" you mean.

Bill is going to assume too that "which" refers to the closest plausible noun, but that may not be what the writer intends. "Healthy eating includes limiting cholesterol and bad fats, which should be the basis of everyone's diet." What is "which"? Healthy eating? The related concept of "limiting cholesterol and bad fats"? Or "bad fats" (we ought to try to eat bad fats?)? Bill can't say. You know, because you wrote it. But Bill doesn't know. How could he? He's not in your head.

Superman

If you keep in mind the relentlessly linear nature of reading, as opposed to writing, you'll avoid the problem of hooking ideas incorrectly that I call a "Superman." My example in class is always this: "Soaring over the rooftops of Metropolis,"—and here I pause and ask the midshipmen, "What word has to come next?" The answer is, of course, "Superman," not—as some writers would have it, "the citizens," as in "the citizens saw Superman." If you are speaking and know where you're going, *you* don't need to have "Superman" as the next word to know that it's not the citizens who are soaring. You already know. But Bill doesn't. Here's another example: "Thinking about the Naval Academy, many things become clear." Who's thinking? The things? The writer knows who's thinking, but Bill doesn't.

11. Awk

One of the funnier professorial shorthands is the overused "Awk," which looks like something related to birds. In fact it usually means "awkward." "Awk" problems almost invariably arise when the writer has failed to remember that s/he isn't going to be reading what's on the page to Bill. In most cases of "awk," the notational system we call writing hasn't reproduced the voice quality necessary to making sense of the statement.

"I will, without really getting my act together, be almost ready in a few minutes." You could *say* this, but you'd need to radically drop your voice between the commas. There's nothing comparable available to the writer to get this effect on the page without re-doing the sentence. Bill reads at the same intensity unless told by the notations of writing to do otherwise, so he has to backtrack to figure out how this fits together. That's "awk."

Parallelism

Grammar books will flash a red light for a sentence like the following. "There are three things I like about Bill: his can-do attitude, his willingness to eat anything, and besides that I am also drawn to the fact that he's a regular guy."

This is what grammar books call "faulty parallelism." It's also an example of an "awk." In Bill's Brand of grammar, I also think of it as part of the common-sense command, "don't confuse Bill."

If something is at the same level as another something, it has to be treated that way. If you start off by saying, "There are three things I like about Bill," you've said you're setting up relationship of equivalence between the three things. The three things have to look the same, like a lineup of three nuts for the same bolt, or three things to insert in the same holder. If the third nut is a different size, it won't fit.

In the sentence above you've ended up saying you "like that you're drawn" to the quality; probably this wasn't your meaning at all. Probably being drawn to is a variation on "liking." Rather than being equivalent to the other two elements, the third one is equivalent to the previous elements plus their connector. These two elements should have been set up as equivalent, rather than as superior and subordinate as they are now set up

Most problems with parallelism are with extraneous parts sticking to elements of the sentence so they won't fit into the holder. "Eat, drink, and [needs third command]—such as "be merry." If you say this: "Eat, drink, and I want to be merry," Bill is simply confused. The holder you've set up accepts things of a certain shape, and so the last thing doesn't fit. Bill is thrown off course. Here the students ask: What do I do to fix this? You might ask this too. In fact, there's usually more than one way to fix a parallelism problem for Bill. You can say either "I want you to eat, drink, and be merry" or "Eat and drink, and I especially want you to be merry." No grammar professor can choose between these: you have to.

You can usually pair two things that don't look the same, because the first one doesn't by itself establish a very strong presupposition of subsequent likeness in Bill. You can write this with no problem: "I like food and going to the gym." It usually takes a series of three things, the first two of which are alike in some fundamental way, to establish in Bill the presupposition that the third one is going to be that way too. But if you go out of your way to imply that two elements are going to be of the same sort, you have to follow through on your implication: To err is human, to forgive divine. Not: To err is human, and God is the only one who can really forgive.

Things can work or fail to work in degrees. The more words you repeat in, say, two elements out of a list of three, the more glaring their absence in the third element becomes. "I want enough money to be independent, enough time to spend it in, and some liberty to do it in would be nice too."

You, the writer, have done this to yourself—and to Bill. You set up a holder of "I want X, Y, and Z," and made X and Y very similar: enough money, enough time. Of course Bill expects Z to be the same, given that X, Y, and Z are set up as being the same. A slightly better version of this is: "I want enough money to be independent, enough time to spend it in, and liberty to do so." No one should mark this one wrong, but it's in the gray area: there's some presupposition that *enough* X and *enough* Y should be followed by *enough* Z, but at least X and Y are followed by Z, so you can probably get away without repeating "enough."

Here's another way of explaining parallelism, and showing how non-parallel elements can confuse Bill. If you set up a situation where the structure leads Bill to expect that things are going to be on the same level, preparing him for two LTs (lieutenants), don't be surprised if he registers pain if you give him an Ensign and an 0-6 (Navy Captain). Here's a mis-match: "People are eating better because of declining prices for vegetables, education is more effective, and changing attitudes have led people to choose the healthy alternative." We don't see what the relationship is between "People are eating better because of declining prices" and "education is more effective." Are these reasons why people are eating better? Unrelated ideas? This is probably going to be marked as a parallelism problem, but it's just as much a punctuation problem (remember, all the elements of grammar are linked). The commas have led Bill to assume that "because of x" will be followed by "[because of] y" and "[because of] z." The writer here has three things which (or that) don't fit together, but the structure of the sentence, with commas and "and," suggests to Bill that they ought to fit together.

All the writer has to do to solve the problem is take away that suggestion. "People are eating better, in part, because of declining prices. Education is more effective than it used to be too. Finally [or: Most important—?], changing attitudes have also led people to choose the healthy alternative." The writer has removed the presupposition that led to the problem by breaking these things apart.

In the following sentence it's clear that the "not" hooks to all three elements of the list: "The law has produced a situation where people are not allowed to move freely, to make their own choices, or even to think." (Alternately, this could read: not allowed to move freely, make their own choices, or even think—because "to" in the first case is assumed to carry over to the other two too.) The reason this is clear is that "not allowed" precedes the first of the three parallel elements, "to move." So it's assumed that it's a holder into which all of the other "to X" elements fits.

In the following sentence, what the modifying word hooks to is unclear. "Literacy has helped people by not keeping them tied to the soil, helping them get better jobs, and freeing their minds." Here Bill's pretty sure that "not" only hooks to the first element because of what the sentence says, but it still slows him down and makes him double back.

"I only feel, think, and live when you're around me." Bill really has to puzzle this one out. If the writer had said "I only feel when you're around me," we have no problems. But the rest of the sentence creates problems. Does the writer mean "only think?" "Only live?" Bill says: "How about, 'The only time I truly feel, think or live is when you're with me'"?

12. Verb tenses

Verb tenses slot actions into time levels: past, present, future. Most of us get the hang of how to use things like "I had been doing this for the last ten years and one day I realized I was sick of it." This whole relationship, the ten years and the realization that followed on them, is in the past. If you're speaking from a point of view right now you say this: "I have been doing this for the last ten years and I am sick of it." Some people who learn English as a foreign language have trouble with these tenses. Many Germans, for example, over-use the progressive ("ing") and say or write "I am living in Annapolis" when they really should say "I live in Annapolis" (what they've said or written implies impermanence or imminent change), or worse, "I am living here since ten years" (rather than "I have been living here for ten years"). When things really get complex, even native speakers have to think. Here are some tenses you might have to think about: "I had been being assaulted every day by publicity, and finally I vowed I would fight back." "Had I thought your reaction might have been different, I would have been more conscious of what I said."

Tense switches

Because slotting actions into time frames is fundamental to establishing chronology, writers have to be careful not to give Bill mis-cues. One way to give him mis-cues is by getting careless and for no good reason changing the slotting. This is comparable to giving your child mixed messages when you're trying to teach him or her good behavior. If you do something differently, because what's happened is an exception, the child has to have a sense for why an exception is an exception, or the discipline doesn't work.

The following is an example of this kind of mixed message, sometimes called a "tense switch." A tense switch isn't intrinsically a bad thing any more than a comma splice is intrinsically a bad thing; it's just that you should want to transmit the information to Bill that it in fact transmits. Most people don't want to transmit this information, and feel exasperated that Bill is on the wrong track. But it's not Bill's fault: he only processes the information he's given.

Tense switches occur when one tense, or time slot, shifts to another. Sometimes this is just what you want to happen. "John told Mark he thinks Bob is a stinker." You've told Bill here that John still thinks Bob is a stinker, right here right now. From just the sentence alone, we can't say whether this is right or wrong. Maybe it's what you want to say; maybe it isn't.

Indirect discourse

Indirect discourse changes what comes out of the bubble in front of my mouth to "He said that ..." The grammar books teach rules of how verb tenses change going from direct to indirect discourse. Usually the books explain that indirect discourse kicks verb tenses back one level: present to simple past, simple past to past perfect. Future turns into conditional ("would").

But the reason this happens is rarely considered, and the gray area people frequently find themselves when deciding how to do this is rarely acknowledged. This gray area may well include "tense switches" you want to happen. Not understanding when they're appropriate means we're left trying to apply a one-size-fits-all rule to a spectrum of possibilities. If we thought of Bill, we'd be able to choose among options, and we'd know why we're making the decision we are making.

The only reason verb tenses change in indirect discourse is that the thing said is no longer true. This may be the case, but it need not be so: you have to look at the situation to tell.

The fact that it's being reported creates a time lag. You have to decide whether the time lag between utterance and reporting changes how you'll express the thing reported. Additionally, in unclear cases, you may have to decide whether you want to emphasize the lag or the thing reported.

Here's what comes out of my mouth: "You have to write for Bill."

"What did he say?" asks an inattentive midshipman.

"He said you have to write for Bill," whispers the fellow sitting next to him. That is, no change in verb form, as you still have to write for Bill.

Similarly, I say: "I'm 6'2 ½."

"What did he say?" asks the midshipman whose attention has wandered.

"He said he's 6'2 ½"." I still am.

If the future is still in the future, no change: "Bill is going to read these tonight."

"What did he say?"

"He said that Bill is going to read these tonight."

It's grammatically possible to follow the pattern and make this "He said that Bill was going to read this tonight." I think this sounds strange.

If the future isn't the future any more, this changes to conditional, or "am going to" changes to "was going to." Here's an example of something I might say:

"Mr. Jones will get the next question because he's trying to sleep."

Five minutes later: "What did he say?"

"He said Jones would get the next question because he was trying to sleep." That "next question" is past; we've long gone on to others.

The same decision process is necessary when you put present tense into indirect discourse. Take this: "I think I'm going crazy." Do you want to emphasize the statement or the fact that it's in indirect discourse? If you want to emphasize it's still true, then use present: "He said he thinks he's going crazy." Use past here if you want to emphasize the pastness of the utterance rather than the presentness of what's being said: "He said he thought he was going crazy." This is confusing, because we don't know if you're telling Bill that the speaker no longer thinks he's going crazy, or whether you're just putting it in indirect discourse. So you'd probably have to explain. The best thing might be to avoid this problem and keep the reported sentence in present unless it happened a long time ago.

If the lag between the utterance and the reporting means the thing said is no longer true, or perhaps not true any longer, you'll want to kick it back a layer in the structure. Present perfect will usually thus become past perfect, but not if it's still true: "I've been here for almost two decades."

"What did he say?"

"That he's been here for almost two decades." Probably not: "He said he'd been here for almost two decades"—though this is grammatically correct.

But: "I've been thinking, and I've decided to give you another opportunity for excellence."

A week passes. "What did he say, you know, last Monday about excellence?"

"He said he'd been thinking, and had decided to give us another opportunity for excellence. That means a quiz."

If the lag in reporting changes the time relationships spelled out within the sentence, that needs to be reflected in the indirect discourse.

"I'm going to be out tomorrow."

"What did he say?"

"He said he's going to be out tomorrow." Or: "He said he was going to be out tomorrow."

The word "tomorrow" doesn't change, because it's still tomorrow with respect to the reporting point of view. But if this isn't so, "tomorrow" has to change. Let's say the indirect discourse reporting happens a week later: We can't say "tomorrow"; we have to say "the next day." Similarly, "yesterday" becomes "the day before," "two days from now" becomes "two days from then," and "two days ago" becomes "two days before."

13. "If" clauses

"If" clauses are examples of patterns you set up that require you to pay attention, because typically they slop over the whole sentence, or even beyond. Here again there are some rule of thumb guidelines about how to construct them; we also need an indication of the gray areas. It's more productive to understand what you're aiming at so you can decide the gray areas than it is to apply the rules without understanding. If you actually understand what you're aiming at, you'll be able to negotiate the gray areas.

Here's an "if" clause: "If I give you the shopping list, will you go to the store for me?"

We put things in conditional to make them more polite, so you get to decide whether you want to say the above, or, instead: "If I give you the shopping list, would you go to the store for me?" Similarly, "Would you like to eat something?" is more polite than "Do you want to eat something?"

"If you thought differently, you should have said so." This means, both of the things are in the past. If the thinking is in the past but the saying could still happen, you will put the second verb form in the present. "If you thought differently, you should say so." It's more likely the person will still be thinking differently, so it would be more likely that you'd say "If you think differently, you should say so." The decision, as always, is made by what you need to convey to Bill.

"If you had thought differently last week, you should have said so." Both the saying and the thinking are last week. But it's also possible, if this is appropriate, to say: "If you had thought differently last week, you should say so" (say now, think then).

Double conditional

"If I give you the money, would you go to the store for me?" The "would" rather than "will" is a sign of politeness. It's used with another person, not with yourself. Many people say something like the following, with a conditional ("would") in both clauses of the sentence: "If I would do X, would you do Y?" Here you are being polite to yourself, emphasizing that you're in some sense being especially charitable to the other person by doing X, or implicitly asking yourself to do it from the position of the other person. Thus it's a mis-cue to Bill.

Say this: "If I had given you the money, would you have gone to the store for me?" Not this: "If I would have given you the money, would you have gone to the store for me?" In the first (don't do) example, we're being faux-genteel to ourselves. It exudes the same kind of fake politeness we get with waiters who indicate something on an object or piece of paper they want us to notice not by pointing with outstretched forefinger but with two fingers, presented slightly curved and with the nails away from us, as if they thought it was impolite to point at a piece of paper as well as at a person. Hey, says Bill, I think we can take it. Just point at the place on the menu, please. And use a normal tone of voice, not that sugary muffled one that's taught as politeness, as if we can't take real speech. (But don't go to the other extreme of informality and address a table full of adults of both sexes as "guys" either, unless it's a sports bar. Maybe not even then. "Ladies and gentlemen" always works.)

14. Mistakes are made

Because of the way sentences are set up, the question of whether something does an action or has an action done to it is fundamental. "Voice" is the way the grammar books express the difference between doing an action and having action done to you. Sometimes the something having action done to it is unspecified. If you express in terms of action do to X, you use the passive voice.

Some grammar gotchas go on crusades against the passive voice. But if the passive voice is what you want, that's what you use. It's just that it's not usually what you want. You have to know what you do want, and that means and you have to know the effect produced on Bill by using each one. A logical question is, Who did it? The default is to tell Bill who did the action. If you're leaving out the actor, there has to be a reason.

The best example I know of a successful use of the passive voice is President Reagan's response to the Iran-contra problems: "Mistakes were made." Here it seems as if the mistakes are the main issue, the people making them minor—or as if the mistakes made themselves. It very carefully avoids blaming anybody, which is surely the point.

It's possible to live completely in the passive voice. The bed was gotten out of, the toilet was used, the teeth were brushed, the toothpaste was squeezed, the eggs were broken sizzling into the frying pan, the coffee was spooned carefully into the coffee machine.

As a bit of literature, this is rather attractive, like a "point of view" movie where you only see what the person sees: Humphrey Bogart before he gets plastic surgery and turns into Humphrey Bogart in the movie *Dark Passage*, for example. All you see is hands and feet, so-called "subjective camera." It creates a strange effect, so that had better be what you want.

We use the equivalent of the passive voice all the time, when we fail to say who the actor is: "I got this shiner in boxing class." "I got" appears active, but it's used in a passive sense: all of a sudden it was there; who gave it to me isn't relevant. There's no functional difference between "somebody in boxing class gave me this shiner" and "I was given this shiner in boxing class," except that nobody says the second one. It seems too formal. You could say it ironically, however: "I was given this shiner as a welcome present in boxing. Like it?"

If you switch from active to passive, or passive to active, you're giving the information that Bill is supposed to see a distinction between the two cases. If he doesn't, he's confused. "John hit Sarah and then Jenny was hit too." Here you're giving Bill the information that it's not so clear John hit Jenny. If that's not the case, you need to fix it. Any particular shift can be justified if that's what you want to tell Bill. "I got up and then was hit in the face by a custard pie." You were in charge until the pie hit from nowhere.

15. Word usage

Picking the right words is as much a part of writing as agreeing subject with verb. Words trail with them their associations, which are the collective history of the way we use them. The more you know about how words are used, the more associations you can evoke. Part of the usage of words consists of knowing who the "we" is who uses them this way: if it's just your immediate world, you have to be aware that outside Bills won't understand them this way.

If you say someone has a "stony" heart, you mean that s/he is unfeeling, unsympathetic. "Stony" is related to the words in the cluster of "cold" and "hard," which indicate someone is impervious to pity, unfeeling. We can thus speak of someone's "ossified" heart, or his/her "petrified" one. The reader understands the connection and probably finds the word choice interesting. But if you say "pebbly" heart (one of my students wrote this and didn't understand why it didn't work), you've entered another cluster entirely. You're out of hardness and into something different. What you're emphasizing now is the uneven texture of the surface, so it implies the person suffers from some sort of heart disease. It seems too you're describing the actual organ of the heart, rather than the metaphoric sense of heart as the source of pity and generosity.

Who makes these clusters? Everybody together. You just have to ask, How do we use these words? If you say "marble" heart to mean unyielding, your usage isn't clear. It falls between clusters. It's close enough to "stone" so that the reader probably gets some sense of pitilessness. But usually when we speak of "marble" we're thinking of the statues made of marble, so it has a sense of "motionless"—it would make more sense to speak of a "marble profile" to indicate someone with an unmoving face: impassive, rather than pitiless. Marble is associated with cold, so it's on the borderline of making sense when applied to the heart. But it's clearly better with the exterior of the body.

Writers who aren't thinking of Bill think that the mere fact they can use a word means it will have for Bill the meaning they associate with it themselves. In their own minds, saying that someone has a "polished" heart suggests polished stone, and so, for them, is telling Bill the person is pitiless. But if you tell Bill someone has a "polished" heart, he's likely to think "good-mannered."

From the perspective of the individual, inside your own head, any usage will seem acceptable. What makes it unacceptable, when it is, is not any quality of the words themselves, but the associations these words have, or don't have. Associations are something you can only get to know by paying attention to how people actually use words.

Langue/parole

The French philosopher of language Ferdinand de Saussure made a distinction between the individual use of language, what he called *parole,* and the collective, what he called *langue.* What was revolutionary for his time was his suggesting that far from being two different types of thing, they were related: if enough individual users changed their *parole,* over time *langue* would change as well.

Some people misunderstood this as a valorization of the individual's right to use language as s/he chose. See? they said? There's nothing intrinsically wrong with my way of saying it: it's just ahead of its time.

But this is wishful thinking. We don't know if it's ahead of its time because we don't know how things are going to play out. Maybe it's just off the beaten path, not on another path. Sure, maybe at some point language will alter to the point where "I are" is acceptable, but I have trouble imagining the changes that English would have to go through to make that possible. In any case, "I are" is clearly a step off the path in what for the present Bill is uncharted territory. And that's all it takes for something to be a mistake.

You can postulate an imaginary, future Bill if you like. You can even write for him. But if he's imaginary and future, you have to be prepared to have no one else get your point in the actual here and now, and perhaps not in the actual future either.

Foregrounding meaning

When we use words we foreground certain aspects of the things they refer to, though the things themselves may have many qualities. Let's go back to the "stony heart." When we say someone "has a stony heart," we're evoking not the whole stone but only certain qualities. We leave aside such things as color (probably the almost-round shape of a stone is why we choose to compare a heart with a stone rather than with other hard things, such as a knife blade) to emphasize that it's unyielding. It would be difficult to make the point that someone was downcast, with a "heavy heart," by saying that s/he had a "stony" heart, though heaviness is just as much a quality of stones as impermeability is. We'd have to say with a "heavy heart." We'd never say, "with a diamond heart," though diamonds are even harder than stones, because so many of the other qualities of diamonds are usually foregrounded, such as visual brilliance. That doesn't mean we can't compare a heart to a diamond. But we'd have to separate out the quality we want, by saying, "her heart was diamond-hard."

There's nothing in the object itself that tells us which of its qualities we're in the habit of foregrounding. If a wobbly writer wrote, "Her heart was money," I don't think Bill would know what s/he meant. If you talk with that person, however, s/he might say: "Oh, I meant it was as good as gold. She was a good person."

"Oh," says Bill. "If you mean gold, you have to say 'gold,' because that's just what we say to mean someone is morally good. We don't say 'money.'"

The wobbly writer may put up a fight. "Why not?" s/he will demand. Gold is valuable, money is valuable. Why can't I say her heart is money just as well as "her heart was gold"?

There's no answer to that except, "That's just not what we say." The point is not that it can't be said, but that you have to do more than just mention the word to foreground the quality you're interested in. You know this by paying attention to how words are used. You can't re-make the world just because a different world would let you do this one thing you want to do. Thinking you can sounds like the rather limp joke about the sixth grader saying his prayers who, after asking divine intervention for his family, adds: "And please make Columbus the capital of Ohio." The father asks why. "Because that's what I put on my geography test!"

It's funny that something so personal, an answer on a test, should be taken as the basis for a request to God—presumably to re-make history, change all the books, everyone's memory and so on—so this one person could do better on a test. But if it seems unjust to the child that Columbus isn't the capital of Ohio, there's no answer possible for the child except, That's just not the way it is. Things are as they are, and if you say something different, you have to be prepared to justify what you've said. After all, that's true of facts too. People generally have two arms, the sky is generally up rather than down, and New York City isn't the capital of New York State, though never so many schoolchildren guess it is. You just have to find out which of those things is true and which isn't. Similarly, you have to pay attention to the way words are used to find out how to use them.

In poems, words are frequently used with their peripheral meanings foregrounded—what we sometimes call connotations, as opposed to denotations, the "dictionary meaning." In fact, denotation and connotation aren't the same kind of thing at all: denotation is simply the overlapping area of many connotation. A good poet can foreground a peripheral meaning and make clear that s/he knows the usage isn't the standard one: the result is like a photograph where the most important object isn't placed front and center. The result can be interesting word usage.

Shakespeare used words in such interesting ways people are still talking about them. Sometimes he's off the main path, but being Shakespeare, he's rarely located in a nowhere, usually (when he's being "interesting") in an almost-somewhere. We might have to listen carefully to pick up the signal, but at least there's not a strong competing signal coming in, so ultimately we do get the right one.

For example, in Sonnet 55 Shakespeare writes: "You shall shine more bright . . ./ Than unswept stone, besmear'd with sluttish time."

Sluttish time? This is initially puzzling. A slut for us is a loose woman, profligate sexually. By extension, however, "sluttish" refers to an entity (here time) with no morality. Time is amoral, in this sense. And, we reflect, "sluttish" also means neglectful of appearance: in disarray. (We have to be aware in reading Shakespeare that the use of words has changed in 400 years, so we'd be well advised to confirm that "slut" had the sense for the Elizabethans of sexual looseness as well.) Both of these senses seem to be evoked here. Time cuts down the good and the bad, and it causes disarray.

The first two lines of the poem deal with "monuments" and "gilded marble," suggesting to the reader that the stone in question is not a stone in the road but a memorial stone. Time that smears the stone of monuments, we realize, *is* amoral, heedless of individuals, and causes loose appearance. The stone is unswept because presumably the passage of time has caused the people to be neglectful, or killed off those who might remember the person memorialized. No sweeping is being done.

I combine a quote with a paraphrase to give the gist of the poem's argument: "When wasteful war shall statues overturn, / And broils root out the work of masonry" (as Shakespeare says, and from here on I continue in my summary), war won't affect the longevity of what people remember about the subject of the poem—as opposed to monuments and statues, because it's captured in the poem, not in stone that decays or is destroyed.

Wasteful war? We pause over this. It doesn't work too well if we think of "wasteful" as a word that applies to someone who spends money or uses too much toilet paper. But it seems to hit the sense of war "laying waste" and also the sense of "waste" meaning profligacy, heedlessness to value. Broils are conflicts, as when we are "embroiled" in something: in the thick of a vast melee. To "root out" literally means to go under the roots: it's not the action of the roots; it means, to go deeply under something. The broils aren't in the ground, they're on the Earth's surface, along with the buildings. But the word usage suggests both that the broils do as effective a job of destroying the buildings as someone who set out to root out the buildings, and that the broils are destroying the buildings almost intentionally.

Here's another example of word usage from Shakespeare. In *Hamlet* (I, ii), Hamlet reacts to the marriage of his mother with his uncle by saying:

How weary, stale, flat and unprofitable
Seem to me all the uses of this world!

> ... 'tis an unweeded garden,
> That grows to seed; things rank and gross in nature
> Possess it merely.

We're struck perhaps first by the fact that Hamlet speaks of the "uses" of the world, as if the world existed only for certain purposes. It suggests too the world has no intrinsic importance, is only a tool for the people who use it. Both are consistent with his jaundiced view of things: the world, as he tells us elsewhere, is "out of joint."

Normally, we'd say the "uses" of the world can't be weary; only a person can be weary. But anything he does makes Hamlet weary, so by extension (and it's Hamlet talking, so misuse is like ungrammatical speech quoted in a novel) the use itself is wary. This use of "weary" is a bit off the beaten path, but doesn't take us to another place entirely. We can still accept the usage, because it's close enough to one we recognize and isn't beginning to be another usage entirely.

"Flat" suggests perhaps flat beer; that's the only negative sense of "flat" that makes sense here. A flat terrain is sometimes boring. But usually we're pleased by a flat terrain, as it's easier to navigate on. To make clear it's boring we have to add some explanation: "it stretches unendingly and unvaryingly as far as the eye can see," we might say.

This would be tweaking the word by giving more context to pull out one particular connotation or peripheral meaning. And in fact this same speech offers an example of Shakespeare doing precisely this: "tis an unweeded garden." If Hamlet had stopped here, Bill (who like his namesake Shakespeare) would probably be simply confused. It's not immediately clear how the world as it seems to Hamlet is comparable to an unweeded garden. If the world *is* an unweeded garden, we might say, his job is to weed it. It's not the most positive thing possible, but it's also not particularly negative. In order to make clear the sense in which Hamlet means an "unweeded garden," Shakespeare has to position it so the sense he needs jumps out. He can't leave it at "unweeded garden."

So he goes on to say, an unweeded garden that grows only "rank [unhealthy, literally rotten but presumably unhealthy in some sense that remains to be defined] and gross [large, ungainly: here's a good example of avoiding later meanings of words in trying to understand a writer]" things that "possess it utterly"—they've taken over, so they seem menacing, with a will of their own—as when we say that the jungle "reclaims" a ruined building and a clearing.

Words need not be used to mean only the things in the overlap area of their denotation, but we have to give them a specific context to pull out non-standard meanings. If you say your dog is "slippery," you'd better immediately explain that you mean "devious, wily" or talk about when he's covered with soapsuds. If you say your bookie is "slippery," people will probably assume "wily" rather than "covered with soapsuds." If you mean the soapsuds, you have to say so, or make some joke about how he's also wily.

Metaphors

A lot of interesting language is metaphoric. But a metaphor isn't a thing clearly separable from other things. We can't make two categories, metaphoric language, and literal language. Instead there's a spectrum with one band being clear metaphors and many things graying into this band and out.

If we say, "his brain is full of trash," we're pretty sure this is a metaphor because we use "trash" primarily to mean household refuse, and we know it can't be in anybody's head. But how about "he changed his mind": is this a metaphor? He didn't exchange one mind (whatever a mind is) for another. How did he change it? But that's simply the way we say that thing. Some people speak of other people as "trash." Is that metaphoric? Or descriptive, meaning human rather than household trash?

If I say, "I have a bone to pick with you," we're pretty sure that's metaphoric: no bones are seen, nor any picked. But if we say, "I want to draw a fine distinction here," is that metaphoric? We're not drawing or making, but isn't that just what we say? Is it metaphoric to call a distinction "fine" (as in a fine point on a pencil)? "I'd like to delineate X from Y"—metaphoric or not? We don't actually get out our ruler to draw a line on the paper, but it can be argued that "to delineate" also means merely "to distinguish." The English "curfew" is a corruption of the French "couvre-feu," which means the hour when the fires are covered and put out. Is the French a metaphor? The English? For both it probably means what it means, namely the time when people have to be off the streets.

The poet Shelley thought that unclear cases like these (metaphor or not?) were dead or dying metaphors: once they had made us sit up straight and pay attention but now were almost completely literal, as we speak of the "table leg" and don't think of flesh and blood. But there's no evidence that "drawing a distinction" between two ideas was ever a "live" metaphor. We don't like to "lose face" and we can tell that somehow it's not literal—nothing is "lost," certainly not our face. But was it ever literal, so that our face fell off? We can understand "face" as what's called a synecdoche, a part standing for the whole ("Washington holds the line on global warming" where "Washington" means "the United States")—or is it metonymy, where one quality is used to stand for the whole, as we make a portrait of a person by painting or sculpting his or her face alone? But how about "lose"? Is it "lose" the way I lose my keys? The way I "lose" my sense of direction? "Lose" my soul? Are the vaguer senses here themselves metonymic with respect to "losing" keys? Things are so complex we can't make clear delineations.

Grammar gotchas are far too fond of making neat maps of language, metaphoric on this side, literal on the other. The reality is much messier. We use phrases in many ways; it's not always possible to identify a primary and a secondary usage, or distinguish literal from metaphoric. All we can say is what works and what doesn't. And that depends on looking at the specific usage after the fact. No set of "how-to" rules will, therefore, ever cover all situations or fix us up in advance. At most we can understand how to judge the effects of what we react, and judge how to react when we find ourselves without a rule. That's the aim of *Bill the Goat's Adult Refresher Guide to Writing*.

Iced drink

A *New Yorker* cartoon by Charles Addams, known for his ghoulish humor, shows two little boys with what seem to be a lemonade stand. The first stand has a sign that says "Iced Drink 5 cents." The second, a bit further down the road, has a sign that says "Iced Drink Antidote $1."

It's funny because the word "antidote" is almost always used in connection with something poisonous, so the suggestion is that these sweet little boys learning capitalism first-hand are willing to murder the passers-by if these don't have or won't pay the $1 to undo the effects of the carefully-labeled "iced drink"—which context would make passers-by (and us) think is lemonade. Perhaps the assumption is, those who've bought the "iced drink" will find the $1 because if they don't the consequences are too dire.

"Antidote" implies "poison." That's what we note from this cartoon. It just does: no one person made this up, that's just the way things are.

Thus if a given John says to a given Jane (or the reverse), "You're my antidote," he's saying that he's noxious or poisonous. I bet that's not what he wants to say at all.

Jane objects, saying, "But you're a good person, John."

"I know I'm a good person," he might insist. "What I meant was that you're my opposite number."

"That's not what you said," objects Jane, who pays attention to how words are used.

"That's what I meant," John insists.

People use words all the time apparently unaware of the meanings the words drag with them. I've had students write about "The Final Solution" with no inkling that post World War II, this phrase now means Hitler's planned extermination of the Jews. I don't think we can say whether this is denotation or connotation; the two merge. This is the way we use this phrase.

John could say: "Jane, I think of you as my antidote, not in the sense of what cures you of the poison—because I think I'm a decent man—but because you're made as my counterpart." Here John is flagging the default, and announcing his intention of going elsewhere.

Jane may still not be convinced. "I still think 'antidote' is too strongly linked to poison, and I don't like thinking of you as poison. Why don't you say I'm the yin to your yang? The cup to your tea?"

John could say: "I think of you as my antidote because on the days when I'm taken over by the blues, you make me happy again." This works better because it makes a distinction between himself and the poison: the poison is *in* him, it isn't *identical to* him. Jane is likely to accept this. I'd say he should have found another word.

We can't say before looking at the word usage if it's within the bounds of the default or not, and whether it has successfully made a path to the default if it's elsewhere. That's the importance of thinking like Bill: Bill can tell you.

D problems

One of the most difficult things to root out among wobbly writers is word usage problems, diction ("D" for shorthand purposes) errors. Let's take a series of examples from students writing about war literature. Many of them contain word usage problems.

It is no question that John is angry. We don't say that. Of course Bill can guess why this could end up in someone's writing. It is very similar to the following, which we *do* say: There is no question that John is angry.

The book is riddled with examples of innocence that is lost. It can be riddled with examples of the loss of innocence, but not of something non-existent or lost: if it's lost it's lost, so it can't riddle.

"Riddle" here, incidentally, means to poke with holes. If all you know is the "joke" meaning, you should at least be puzzled, and realize: there must be another meaning; I should look it up.

The idea is started that they are now old. Bill can't even guess what this means. Someone *introduces* the idea that they are old? The idea is *floated*? This could also be a passive/active problem: if the writer were forced to tell Bill who "started" the idea he might have to get the right verb—clearly "start" isn't what we need.

One of these perceptions or normalities that has been shed is modesty. Modesty isn't a perception, and Bill has no idea what a "normality" is here. In any case, we can't shed either a perception or a "normality."

The ability to kill is antithetical to innocence. How is an ability antithetical to a quality? Perhaps: The ability to kill makes innocence impossible(?).

History and media, fall short when accurately describing what war is really like. First off, get rid of the comma. Then the writer has said that history and media *do* accurately describe what war is like, but in doing so fall short—whatever that means. Fall short of accuracy? But see "when accurately describing." Probably he means "fall short of accurately describing." Why are "history and media" paired? Are these different? The same type of thing, things that can be paired?

the pointless and trivial nature of war. Pointless nature? Surely "pointlessness." "Trivial nature"? Trivial means so unimportant we don't even waste time with it. That's not the same as "pointless."

They are unmotivated and apathetic towards Germany's cause. You can be "apathetic towards" something, but not "unmotivated towards" it. (Incidentally, American usage prefers "toward" while British prefers "towards.") This is one of those nut and bolt problems: the writer has to separate off "unmotivated" with a comma: that way the "towards" hooks only to "apathetic."

The soldiers have personal debts against one another. We don't do that in English. At most the soldiers can have "personal grudges."

The trivial point is that the armies on both sides hunt and kill an enemy that they see as an enemy for an invalid reason. If the point is trivial, don't make it. "An enemy that they see as an enemy"? Are there enemies that they don't see as enemies? Possible, but it needs to be spelled out. A reason can only be good or bad, not valid or invalid: an argument is valid, of which a reason can be a part.

One more insight as to how pointless war is. We don't say "insight as to." We say "insight on" or "insight to understanding."

His life is lost for a hopeless case. This is ballparking, and the words aren't even complex: "A hopeless cause."

The main problem that the character has is the innocence, mainly his, that has been destroyed by the war. The problem isn't his innocence, which in any case has been destroyed. It's the destruction. So: "The character's main problem is his inability to deal with the war's destruction of both his own innocence and that of his fellow soldiers."

16. *Nobody's perfect*

These items make a lot of balls to keep in the air at the same time, many things you have to think about simultaneously. Do the best you can, but don't beat yourself up when you drop some of these balls from time to time. Everybody does, including me. I've read over this manuscript countless times: every time I catch another problem or two. Writing is hard, because it goes against the grain: it's not about how things feel to us, but how they look to Bill. Nobody is going to be able to see everything s/he does from Bill's perspective all the time, because nobody but Bill is Bill (Bill doesn't write, so he doesn't have to worry about writing for another Bill). Becoming a better writer doesn't mean never writing things you later realize to be unclear. It means getting more of them clear to begin with, and knowing a problem when you see it on re-reading.

IV
Correcting Your Own Course

If you write for Bill, that means you correct your course continually, focusing on the goal you've defined. You get individual words back on course, sentences, paragraphs, even whole sections of your writing. You do this while you write, and you do it after you write.

Here's what it looks like for Bill to correct when the writing has gone off course.

1. Student papers

For students, the hole they're trying to fill is the assignment. For other writers, it will be the parameters set by a boss, or their own sense that something is needed, something they have to define. Here's the assignment for this paper, so we can follow along the attempt of the writer to fill this hole:

Your paper topic is: "The Most Unexpected Aspect of Plebe Summer." Two pages, about 600 words.

First, you need to find an aspect that someone who didn't experience it will be interested in reading about. NB: An "aspect" is not the same as an event, though an event can allow you to see an aspect. Look these two words up if you don't understand. In the course of the essay, you'll have to give Bill some sense of who you are and why this particular thing should have struck you; perhaps ruminate on its implications. At the same time, avoid getting side-tracked in personal anecdotes that are much more interesting to you than to Bill.

Aim for clarity of thesis and elegance of development. Do not merely give me a series of disjointed observations; on the other hand do not limit yourself to describing something that happened. I do NOT want one of the 5-paragraph essays you may have learned to do in high school. These are better than nothing, but at the college level we have to get more sophisticated. DO NOT begin by saying "In this paper I will be making three points"; do not begin "body" paragraphs by saying "My next point is X"; do not tack on a useless paragraph (the fifth under the rules of the 5-p-e) repeating what I already know: "In this paper I have shown that X, Y, and Z." EVERY paragraph gives new information. DO give the information the 5-paragraph essay gives, but do it more subtly. This is college, not high school.

And now they're on their own. Part of the aim here is that the students need to see the distinction between what they have to do and what's up to them. Understanding this distinction is the way they decide what the size of the hole is, and it's the way they see that many decisions just don't matter in writing. Bill doesn't care.

Bill doesn't care what your aspect is, so long as it's an aspect. He does care if it's an event you're talking about: say, the fact that you did better on a run than you'd expected to. (This could be parlayed into an aspect: that the physical demands of the summer were more reasonable than you'd expected.) One midshipman's "most unexpected aspect" of plebe summer was the low level of hygiene, leading to rashes and funguses (time for showers is limited to non-existent). For another, the most unexpected aspect of plebe summer was the fact that he had no free time.

The title this particular writer gave his paper was "Invisible Challenges." That suggests, challenges that no one on the outside can see, things he struggled with inside and gave no sign of to others. Is this what his paper would be about? Bill registered the presupposition and waited to see. This, below, was the first paragraph, with Bill's reactions (many thanks to the author, one of my favorite midshipmen, who agreed to let me use his work to show others how to write for Bill as well):

As I got out of the car on the street leading to Alumni Hall, millions of thoughts were surging through my head. Where is Alumni Hall? Bill's home is the stables and the football field, not the main buildings. Was he even at the Naval Academy? My plebe knew, but wasn't thinking that he might have to tell Bill. Was this perhaps—Bill is taking a wild guess here—where newly arrived plebes went first on their arrival at the Academy? If so, why not tell Bill that? **One of these thoughts was that I had better not be late for my Induction day**

reporting time but other thoughts involved how I was going to deal with the yelling and how well I would transfer from being a civilian to becoming a military officer. If "Induction" is capitalized, "Day" needs to be capitalized too. My plebe needs a comma after "but." Otherwise it sounds as if the writer is just shouting it all out in one breath, the way the plebes do their "chow calls," lightning speed versions of the day's menu and the officers of the watch. Other thoughts didn't "involve" how etc.; they *were* these things. Why "but"? The second and third thoughts don't pose a contrast with the first, they're just different thoughts. "Transfer from"? Sounds as if he's going from one place to the other, not one situation to another. He may have meant "transition from." Why link being X with becoming Y? This transition can be instantaneous, as the process of becoming an officer begins with the first moment. Perhaps: "transition from being civilian to being a military officer." **I became a deer in headlights and Alumni Hall was the vehicle barreling towards me.** This expression of a "deer in the headlights" is frequently applied to plebes. But Bill, who has other concerns than plebes, might not know this and would need him to follow it with something like this: "a frequent comparison for plebes." (Note: "A deer in the headlights," or "a deer-in-headlights plebe": if all those words precede their noun they need to be hooked together with hyphens so Bill knows *as he reads* that they belong together and to expect the noun after them. After the noun, after he's doubled back and tripped, isn't soon enough.) Bill gets a good laugh out of the image of Alumni Hall, which sounds like and indeed is a large substantial building, barreling toward anybody. Why is it the building that's so scary? We've already gone from Alumni Hall to the thoughts; now we're back at Alumni Hall again. **I knew it would be a long day, but when I looked at Alumni Hall, I had no idea that the vehicle speeding towards me was an eighteen wheeler.** Having a building coming toward you is much worse than being in the path of an eighteen-wheeler (NB: written with a hyphen to make clear these two words together, neither of which is a noun, make up your object). Besides, if Alumni Hall is barreling down on him, it's not an eighteen-wheeler, it's a building. The real problem here is the metaphor of the building bearing down on this plebe: fix that by getting rid of it. **Plebe summer would present me with many challenges; I felt that every bullet I had anticipated was only a distraction in comparison to homesickness, the indoctrination**

process, and the military bearing and respect I would learn. The time shift here is awkward: we go from the moment before beginning plebe summer to a kind of wrap-up mode. The metaphor shifts from a building barreling down on him and him the deer to someone being shot at. In what sense are these bullets "a distraction"? Probably he means "unimportant." The list of things that were presumably more important consists of three things that don't seem to go together. Homesickness is something he feels, the indoctrination process is something he's being subjected to, and both "military bearing" and "respect" are things he says from his distanced perspective that he learned, one external and one internal.

But Bill's most pressing question is: How is this filling the required hole? How does it connect to the topic? What is the topic sentence?

The next paragraph is a far too long re-evocation of what it was like to take part in the Academy's week-long summer seminar, which is otherwise unidentified to Bill. The final sentence of this paragraph, by now more than halfway through the paper, might serve as a topic sentence of the paper. The idea is introduced some three sentences before the paragraph's end (a bad place for something this important). The plebe tells Bill that his father had had a military career. Then: **His hard work and determination helped him get through the worst of times, so I used his strength to overcome my weakness. I never thought I would rely on my dad's Navy career to help me with my Navy career.** There are a number of things unclear here, but Bill, who has seen no topic sentence for the first half of the paper and who, were he not paid to read this, would long ago have given up, jumps on what seems a response to the question. Here, at last, is something that was unexpected, and a veritable aspect: "I never thought I would rely on my dad's Navy career" etc. To be sure, it's unclear in what way the writer is "relying" on his father's "career"; probably in fact he's relying on the strength produced by thinking about his father's career. Nor does he tell Bill that his father in fact exhibited hard work and determination, or justify, even fleetingly, the statement that these helped the father get through the "worst of times" (such as what?). But it's better than what was there before.

What a horror: a whole page having no idea where things are going. In the case of an assigned paper or a piece of writing for the job, the reader, Prof. or Boss Bill, knows what the size of the hole is: s/he knows what the task or assignment was and can be aware that what s/he is reading isn't the peg to fill this hole.

Here's another paper that's supposed to be responding to the same cue. Here the writer has started filling a hole, but it's not the one he's supposed to be filling. Or rather, it turns out to be several holes. Remember the topic: "The Most Unexpected Aspect of Plebe Summer." This writer too liked the idea of sharing his false start.

With graduates like Fleet Admiral Nimitz, Admiral Stockdale, and Senator McCain, there can be little argument as to whether or not the Naval Academy serves as an effective training center for future naval officers and leaders. Let's start with the mid-to-low level problems, the things that kick Bill in the shins. The first is a Superman. "With graduates like X, Y, and Z," has to be followed by the thing that this modifies. The pattern looks like this: With friends like that, who (the person with the friends) needs enemies? Or: With a face like that, you (the person with the face) could be a model. "Little argument as to whether or not." The argument isn't "as to whether or not," it *is* whether or not. The phrase "as to" is followed by the quality you think there's no question of, as in "There can be little question as to the Naval Academy's effectiveness as an institution to train leaders." Bill isn't thrilled with the logic here: three graduates over many decades do not a summer make. How typical are they? Do they have anything in common other than their notoriety? If so, Bill needs to hear about it. "With graduates who have shown tenacity in the face of adversity like X, Y, and Z,"—how can this go on without being logically assailable? Perhaps: "The Naval Academy has shown it can produce people with The Right Stuff." That's about as strong a claim as you can be allowed here.

More seriously, Bill is worried on other counts. This doesn't seem anywhere near the hole we need to be filling. We're told this fact is certain, so there's not going to be room for a surprise here. What's it going to be?

However, before coming to the Naval Academy, I did not fully process the fact that the Naval Academy produces *junior* officers "who have *potential* for future development." (Author's italics). Suddenly we're in subjective territory: the writer is telling Bill what he knew (in the writer's terms, what facts he "processed"). The sentence before spoke of whether or not there was argument about something. The problem is lack of parallelism, or perhaps a missing antecedent to "facts." You compare facts with facts, not presence or absence of argument with facts. The writer could go back to the previous sentence and use the word "fact" so its relationship to the next sentence is clear. "It's a fact that the Naval Academy can produce leaders, as we see from X, Y, and Z." The logic of this sentence, in any case, has Bill's brow furrowed. Surely all these now-senior men were at one point junior officers with potential for development. How is their existence on the Earth a contrast to this idea? Why is "however" justified? Worst of all, Bill's worry that the first sentence didn't fill the hole of "Most Surprising Aspect of Plebe Summer" has not gone away. To be sure, this sentence suggests something the writer didn't know. That's to the good. But it's difficult to see how a realization that junior officers have potential is going to translate into an aspect of plebe summer. **In essence, the Naval Academy lays a foundation of leadership that Midshipmen can then take with them after graduation and build upon throughout their careers.** This sentence doesn't make things exponentially worse, even if doesn't make them any better. Clearly it's continuing the idea of the previous sentence; the fact that Bill sees a connection is good. However, the image of laying a foundation is of constructing an immovable frame of stone in the ground; it's not something midshipmen will be able to "take with them after graduation." On the positive side, foundation is the same image as "build upon." A truly mixed metaphor would have had midshipmen perhaps "cashing in" on the foundation or "taking inspiration from" it.

Consequently, the system places young men and women with little leadership or "real-world" experience in charge of the indoctrination and training of the 4/C Regiment. Consequently? What's this hook to? Because the Naval Academy "lays the foundation"? Because Midshipmen "take a foundation with them after graduation"? Probably the first, since the second doesn't work at all. Perhaps the writer wants something like "In order to make this foundation firm"—merely repeating "lay the foundation" is worse, but at least fills the bill. Doing X in order to achieve Y is a different logical relation than doing Y as a consequence of Y. **I never would have imagined that the upper-class could be just as new to the training environment of Plebe Summer as I was.** Bill sees that this at least offers something unexpected ("I would never have imagined") and so has to be filling the right hole. But how does the writer get here from where he started? The logic seems flipped: if he'd started with this sentence, Bill would be with him. What precedes it seems to be developing a different idea entirely. Namely, giving a reason why it's not surprising he'd have been surprised: it's not a vital idea, and certainly shouldn't come first; probably the writer doesn't need it at all. He's anticipating an objection that isn't likely to come. Something on the order of: You dummy, why were you surprised that the upper-classmen in charge of Plebe Summer were inexperienced? Apparently the writer is making the rueful admission that all he'd heard or thought about when he considered the Naval Academy was a handful of its most celebrated, successful, and older graduates. He'd never thought of the process necessary to making people like that. Now *this* is something Bill understands, but this idea isn't on the page—at least not without connecting more dots than are actually there. And in any case it comes, if at all, after the topic sentence.

Now it may seem absurd that the upper-class, who have already completed three years at the Academy, could be placed in the same environment as me, and be just as disoriented as I was. Bill supposes it *may* seem absurd, but the fact is, it isn't likely to. The writer is reacting to an objection that Bill would never make, perhaps because he doesn't understand the writer's point. What's absurd about upperclassmen (in midshipman terminology, "the upper-class") being "placed in the same environment" as the writer? Isn't the environment the Naval Academy? And what's surprising about that? The rest of the sentence is more promising: "absurd that the upper-class could be just as disoriented as I was." The thing the writer finds surprising is that the upper-class were (for lack of a better word) incompetent, or perhaps merely young and inexperienced (it's unclear at this point what he's saying about them). Bill, he says, may think this odd. But Bill doesn't know enough to think it's odd: perhaps from the star-struck perspective of a plebe who has to say "Sir" and "Ma'am" to anything that moves that's larger than a dog, the idea that the upper-class should be young/inexperienced/incompetent is surprising. But if that's the point, the writer needs to say that. "As a newly-arrived plebe at the Naval Academy, I assumed the upper-class in charge of Plebe Summer would be gods, as fully formed as leaders as the heroes who had brought me to Annapolis: X, Y, and Z." Perhaps the next sentence would be something like this: "What I didn't realize was that even X, Y, and Z, had to start somewhere, and that the surprisingly low level of leadership shown by the upper-class was where they had undoubtedly started." **But one must keep in mind that when they went through Plebe Summer, they too were lost, scared, and confused.** It's unclear to Bill where this sentence is going. Why do we have to keep this in mind? **It was assumed that they knew nothing and they were treated accordingly.** This seems a new idea, but isn't flagged as one. Their being lost, scared, and confused is somehow related to their being treated as if they knew nothing. Is knowing nothing the same as being lost, scared and confused? Perhaps the point is that they actually did know something. However because they were lost, scared and confused, their own leaders assumed worse of them than they should, namely that they knew nothing. This lack of knowledge was perpetuated because— and here Bill falls silent. Because what? "Accordingly" doesn't help. If they knew nothing, treating them "accordingly" might be telling them many things to make up a perceived gap. Here it probably means, No attempt was made to teach them. But this doesn't follow. **However, this time, going through Plebe Summer as Cadre, they were expected to be leaders, trainers, and teachers.** "However" throws Bill. Perhaps: despite the fact that they had never been treated as potential leaders, they were suddenly expected, after the mere passage of three years (in which no one treated them differently than they had been treated in Plebe Summer?), to be leaders for the newly arrived plebes. **They were to set the example and serve as role models for the Plebes.** Bill thinks he may be on a scent here; this is what he now expects. **Yet, for many of them, Plebe Summer Detail is the first time that they are put in a leadership position with such responsibility. When were they supposed to learn these skills; and from who?** The ideas are all here, they're just in the wrong order. And it should be "from whom" (see below). Here's a more logical order, and Bill's best shot at a re-write:

The biggest surprise Plebe summer held in store for me was finding the upper-class such weak leaders. My surprise was certainly the result of my own naïvite, my visions of joining an institution peopled by mature statesmen and Admirals—who were the only names I had to associate with Annapolis. I'd forgotten that great leaders can be made, not just born, and failed to ask how typical they might be, even in younger form, of the Academy's many midshipmen. Why, I later wondered ruefully, should upper-classmen in fact be better leaders than scared plebes? I subsequently came to realize that until they are given Plebe Summer assignments, the upper-class have no opportunities to practice leadership. That's what they do in Plebe Summer. No wonder it was a learning process for all.

But this may not be what the writer intended. By way of excusing the upper-class for their incompetence, it now openly asserts what's implied before, namely that there are no leadership opportunities before Plebe Summer. Bill thinks this probably isn't true, and in any case how would a plebe in his second week after Plebe Summer be in a position to say this? The writer is merely speculating; if by contrast he's not speculating and has evidence to back up his assertion, he hasn't offered it to Bill—he needs to do so.

"From who?" that ends the sentence makes Bill feel as if he's bitten on aluminum foil with a mouthful of fillings. If the fact that you need the objective case of "who," namely "whom" is de-emphasized, it's not an issue—that's where Bill is a pragmatist, and agrees with those who find the grammar gotchas all a bit too harpy-like. If the need for "whom" is buried, then sure, leave off the "m." However following "from," set off by a comma on one side and a period/full stop on the other, this one is very exposed. You've set it up and then refused to do it correctly. This is the time to use "whom."

Bill is pretty disoriented, because he got off to a bad beginning. However he's on something like a predictable course by now: he sees that what was surprising was that the "cadre," as they're called (one of them is "a cadre" [!]) weren't very good. So he's expecting to follow this course for a while. Does he get to do so? He's hopeful, because the question at the end of the last paragraph, despite his wince, at least appears to be setting up the following paragraph. This ending was what appeared a rhetorical question: Where are they supposed to learn leadership? Given that it's implied the upper-classmen have no opportunity to learn leadership before they're thrown into their roles as "cadre," it seems the answer to this is, "nowhere." So does the following paragraph link to this ending? Let's see.

At the Naval Academy, Midshipmen get their "hands on" experience while serving in the positions that they have been assigned to learn. At a place like Recruit Training Command, Great Lakes, or at any of the Navy Vocational Schools, the training positions are held by experts who have had many years of experience in their field. Bill is once again seriously knocked off course. He doesn't see how this idea links to the previous one. In fact, it seems to contradict the implication that Midshipmen have no opportunities for leadership—unless the point is, leading in Plebe Summer after three years as a Midshipman is precisely the sort of hands-on training the writer was referring to above. But here the point has to be not that they get this training, but that they get none before they are abruptly thrown in at the highest level and asked to do the things they will in fact be doing later on. The sentence that follows in the essay only makes sense if Bill adds a sentence in the middle, something that contrasts the Naval Academy way of doing things to the Recruit Training Center or the Vocational Schools. But even here Bill is still confused: are these experts the contrast to the inept/inexperienced upper-classmen who do such a bad job with the plebes? Or are the people who give aspiring leaders like the upper-class the instruction that, according to this writer, is missing at Annapolis?

When I first noticed this arrangement, my initial reaction was that the system provided a great disservice to the 4/C Midshipmen, depriving us of the first-rate training that we could receive from a qualified instructor. Aha, says Bill. At least this answers the question he had above. Of course, keeping Bill in the dark for even as long as it takes to read a sentence is not a good thing; it means he stumbles along for that long, feeling abandoned and weary. The beginning of this sentence doesn't help Bill: "this arrangement"? He's trying to figure out what arrangement is meant: the arrangement at the Naval Academy? Or at Great Lakes? If Great Lakes, what is this realization doing here in this paper? Tell Bill first that the writer went to Navy Recruit Center and saw something different than he later saw at the Academy. If the Naval Academy, it's too late in the paper: we've already had the writer noticing it. **Yet, as I gave it more thought, and as I realized that this institution is designed to produce quality *potential* leaders, the system seemed more appropriate.** Oh. So the Naval Academy. So the point really has to be that the writer now understands the purpose of this USNA system. How does this link to the question of the most unexpected aspect? It's an idea that perhaps could be mentioned as an aside in the first paragraph—to show that surprise later turned to acceptance—but in any case would be developed only later. And Bill is still lost with this thing about producing (as Ensigns?) potential leaders—apparently as opposed to actual ones. Is the idea that you're not supposed to graduate from the Naval Academy with any real skills, but only the capability of learning some? If so, it's an odd one, and it seems unlikely to Bill, who after all has read many papers by plebes in his time, that this is where the writer is really going.

At a Navy Vocational School or at Recruit Training Command, there are specific skills and knowledge that must be imparted upon the sailors. Come on, says Bill. Tell me that you went to one of these! Bill is catching on that the writer is a "prior," a prior-enlisted sailor. But the writer hasn't told him. There's a glimmer of a contrast introduced here: the emphasis of this sentence is somehow on specific skills and knowledge. Presumably the writer is going to contrast that with something that's not specific. Bill, by now pretty disoriented, hopes the writer will in fact do so. He's not heartened by the strange phrase "imparted upon"—in English, we don't "impart upon," we "impart to." **Here at the Naval Academy, the main focus is learning the art of leadership.** Bill by now has largely lost the sense of where he's going, but he's grateful that at least this small part of the path is clear to him. This does seem to be a contrast, precisely the one we needed: leadership vs. skills. How it links to the surprise has largely gone by the wayside. **Naval officers do not have to know how to setup a telecommunications link, or strip, sand, and paint a bulkhead.** Enough of the road blocks and Bill isn't even asking where he's going, he just wants to be put out of his misery. A "setup" is a noun, frequently a kind of trap, like a frame as in "I was framed" (images of the non-speaking Marx Brother Harpo with his ridiculous head of blonde curls come to mind, ferociously carving a square into the air that Groucho, complete with glistening painted-on stripe-standing-for-moustache, immediately interprets, correctly, as "I'm being framed"). A setup isn't a verb; the verb is "to set up."

As Bill reads, he has other "issues" (as we say) as well. Here's the sentence again: **Naval officers do not have to know how to setup a telecommunications link, or strip, sand, and paint a bulkhead.** Bill, as we know, processes in a linear fashion. Naval officers do not have to know how to G an H, or—what is Bill expecting here? Let's stop the sentence and find out. The sentence could continue: or an I, or a J (that is, how to G an H, an I, or a J). Or the "or" could signal this kind of a sentence: "how to G an H, or I it" (that is, how to G an H or an I). As he reads he's trying to figure out how much of the first part of the structure carries over to the second. The problem with this sentence is that it takes him to the end to figure out. It could be, "do not have to know how to set up a telecommunications link, or strip, sand and paint one." It's unclear what that means, but Bill has to process the structure before he tries to figure out if he understands the sense. In fact, what's being stripped, sanded, and painted is another object. Bill could be spared the microseconds of confusion by a sentence like this: *Naval officers do not have to know how to setup a telecommunications link, or how to strip, sand, and paint a bulkhead.*

Instead officers must learn how to supervise, motivate, counsel, and maximize their subordinates. Bill likes the fact that this completes the structure of Naval officers do not do X, they do Y. However he's not quite sure how the assertions work here. Officers must learn, fine. But how? This once again seems to say that merely being an officer implies no particular skill as an officer; you're an officer, then you learn how to be one. This may be what the writer is saying—though it seems unlikely—but he hasn't said it. Bill likes all the verbs applied to "subordinates" except the last. Maximize your subordinates? Maximize what? Their subordination? **Therefore, it is not so important that Midshipmen become proficient in any specific field, but instead, that they learn how to adapt to unexpected situations, lead confidently and deliberately, even when they are unsure of the outcome, and to always strive to acquire more knowledge and experience to develop into more effective leaders.** Bill is ready to throw in the towel. It seems we're hearing that once officers become officers, they learn leadership. Now we're hearing that it's important that by the time midshipmen are officers they have these skills. "Therefore" doesn't work: it's an overreach. What does learning how to adapt to unexpected situations have to do with anything that's preceded it?

The sentence causes Bill to trip in the middle of feeling he's completely off the track again. It's set up like this: "It's important that they X, Y and Z." The problem is that after the Y, instead of giving a Z that looks like the X and Y (adapt, lead), we get something that looks quite different, "to always strive." This is faulty parallelism, but the real issue is that Bill is expecting all the steps to have the same height, called a rise: if you set up expectations, you have to fulfill them. If you want a different rise on the staircase, make it that way from the beginning of the steps so we don't trip in the middle.

To repeat a point made above: when you do split the two elements of the infinitive ("to boldly go where no man has gone before") Bill is going to notice the word in the middle. If the word in the middle doesn't justify that degree of attention, don't do it. Here I'd say it doesn't justify that degree of attention. I think the writer is saying officers-to-be have to strive to acquire knowledge and experience. The point is striving to acquire. The focus shouldn't be on always striving; that's implied by "striving," and it's not contrasting with striving sometimes. So Bill doesn't see the point. An example where it makes sense to split an infinitive is this: "I hope to always love you." Here the emphasis is on the "always," so it's correctly put in the middle of the unit, where we'll be sure to see it. **Until recently, I did not fully realize or understand the true mission of the Naval Academy, but now, since becoming member of the Brigade, it has become more apparent to me why this institution exists, and I am proud to be a part of it.** The focus has shifted from the surprising aspect to the world beyond the surprise, the explanation of the thing the person initially found surprising. When in any case is "recently"? We haven't understood enough of the "mission" to have the writer refer to "the true mission" and be able to nod our heads (to make people who are leaders? Who can, once they become officers, become leaders?). Why do we care that the writer knows why this institution exists? It's "motivating" (as we say at Annapolis) that he wants to be part of it, but Bill, by this point, has given up. He's a bloodied heap by the side of the road, nursing his bruises and wondering why he ever agreed to go on this run.

After

If they think of Bill as they revise, writers can learn to fix their own mistakes. This writer and I had an EI session, where we Billed his paper. This is the result. Bill likes this one much better.

False Presumptions

("presumption" isn't wrong, but "presupposition" is more usual and is probably what he was aiming at: we can have the "presumption of innocence," which can be false, but it's unusual to see this usage in the plural, whereas it's quite common with "presuppositions")

As I struggled through Plebe Summer, I could not help but notice that my Cadre seemed to be just as unfamiliar with their new positions as I was with mine. I began to realize that I was not the only one who had been immersed in a new and unfamiliar

environment. They too were being put through rigorous training and the only real difference between them and I [it's in objective case, so it should be "me"] was the type of training they were receiving. My pre-I-Day assumptions were that the Cadre would be the equivalent of a Marine Corps Drill Instructor; [should be ":"] daunting, pitiless, and omnipotent. Yet it was evident from the very beginning that this was not the case.

As I observed my Cadre throughout each day I was almost always able to perceive a hint of uncertainty or uneasiness about them. They never seemed completely settled into their positions and it [this?] was most noticeable in their dialogue and inconsistent behavior.

Whether we were being reprimanded or praised, the things the Cadre said hardly ever seemed sincere. Their reprimanding was typically so far-fetched and unreasonable that it was ignored, and their praising was always so cliché and scripted that it seemed forced (almost as if they were basing their actions and comments off of some sort of leadership formula or checklist). Thus, we either really are America's best and brightest or those Interpersonal Relationships Briefs we attended over the summer were more effective than I thought, for, [comma out] it was always obvious to my shipmates and me when the Cadre were being straight with us and when they were just putting on an act. Consequently, we eventually stopped taking their empty threats and motivational phrases seriously, which had a significant negative impact on our level of performance.

In addition, they failed to employ one of the most fundamental aspects [employ an aspect?] of quality leadership. When interacting directly or indirectly with subordinates, it is crucial to display a consistent leadership type [not display a type, display leadership of a certain type]. Whether it be one of firmness and stoicism, or gentleness and compassion, it is important to stay relatively constant. Our Cadre would be cracking jokes and "loosening up" one second, and would be making us do rack races and motivational PT the next. I understand that Plebe Summer is designed to teach us how to cope with a constantly changing environment, but the Cadre's behavior would change from relentless trainers to college seniors, and end up as friendly shipmates. With such varying personas, it is nearly impossible to trust their intentions and abilities [make clearer the personas (as we now say; better is "personae") in question were those of the "Cadre"; we don't trust abilities, we trust that people have them].

As one might imagine, I was very taken aback by the things I witnessed over Plebe Summer. Here, they [we've lost who "they" is] struggled to motivate a group of misfit Plebes, and yet, in less than one year the Cadre will be giving orders to enlisted personnel (who could have as many as twenty years of naval service). At first I looked on with disbelief, but as time progressed, I soon became frustrated, and even reached the point at which I was disappointed with their performance. All one has to do is look around the yard to see countless examples of Midshipmen who have a considerable lack of experience in leadership accompanied by a false sense of confidence. As an idealistic newcomer, I failed to contemplate the possibility that Naval Academy Midshipmen are not finished products upon graduation.

With minor mistakes, it's pretty close to all there. Bill can, for once, relax.

2. Newspaper article

It's painful for writers to see how badly they mislead Bill, but necessary. Some writers will never know. The following appeared in a publication of the Naval Academy, an official government newspaper (and hence in the public domain). It's just a human interest article, so probably not too much of Bill's functional time is lost as a result of its getting off course. But other government writing could result in huge inefficiency in the machine. I'm starting at the beginning and then skip for the sake of concision.

Tourists glimpsed at what Fort McHenry might have looked like almost 200 years ago during the Battle of Baltimore when a sea of midshipmen in their summer white uniforms entered the fort's grounds to take a tour recently. This starts with a D problem: we don't say "glimpsed at." The whole sentence implies that midshipmen visited the Fort during the Battle of Baltimore. Presumably the author's point, unclear until Bill reads below, is that the sheer number of people in the ruined Fort approached the number of people who would have been there during the Battle of Baltimore. How 700 (as we later learn) 18-year-olds, short-haired men and women, dressed in white uniforms, could approximate long-haired 18th century male soldiers dressed quite differently—and how many of these were there?—is unclear too. Probably the author was just trying to get in an echo of history by evoking the military predecessors of the visitors, and suggesting that the midshipmen were somehow like the soldiers during the Battle of Baltimore because they too are military, and numerous. These common qualities might function as links, but they'd have to be spelled out better. Here they seem too weak.

The plebes marched in ranks to different stops throughout the fort. They visited the Water Battery, toured the fort and talked about the flag, the "Star Spangled Banner" and the Battle of Baltimore.

The midshipmen brought the old fort to life, said XX [my change; the original contains a real name], one of Fort McHenry National Monument and Historic Shrine's park rangers. "The tourists love seeing the midshipmen tour the fort," said X. "It was just neat to see the volume of the different companies as they marched in. Just the sheer numbers of midshipmen really gave the fort a living quality, an active military presence and that is one thing that a lot of people commented on that made a really positive impression on the visitors."

The quotes don't seem to be given in proper sequence. The second, about tourists' reactions, doesn't follow from saying that the midshipmen brought the Fort to life. Even if the speaker actually uttered his remarks in this order, they cause Bill to wrinkle his brow when reported in the same order. The newspaper article's author needs either to switch them around, or eliminate the quote that doesn't fit with the others (standard journalistic practice). After all, the second quote, "tourists love etc." isn't necessary at all, as it's implied later.

The speaker could profitably pay more attention to what he says: it's not the volume of the *different* companies that's "neat," presumably, but their collective volume. The different volumes of the various companies? No, because companies are about the same size.

It wasn't just the numbers that impressed onlookers, X said. It was a combination between that, midshipmen's behavior and just the interest they had in learning about the history of the fort and the Navy.

The previous paragraph has in fact said it was the sheer number of midshipmen that impressed onlookers, so this reads like a retraction, confusing to Bill. The author of the article needs to consolidate the points of view and report the sum at the top. If this new point is a caveat to the earlier one, it needs to be presented as such. The earlier paragraph also needs to be ratcheted back a bit to allow a caveat later: "To some degree, it was the volume" etc. That prepares Bill for this new idea, which should start with "But" or "However."

D problem: we don't say "a combination between," we say "a combination of."

"We could only do a tour like that with a group as well trained as a military unit like the Naval Academy midshipmen," said X. "To give over 700 people a tour over the course of an entire afternoon and have it go as smoothly as it did is a remarkable testament to the midshipmen and their discipline."

Once again x should be thinking more carefully about what he says. His sentence has a compound subject: one half is "to give over 700 people a tour," the other is "have it go . . . smoothly." These collectively require "*are* a remarkable testament," not "is." But in fact his real subject is only the second one. He should have said: "To have a tour with this many people go so smoothly is a testament etc." He's focusing on the smoothness of the numbers he's focusing on, not the numbers and the smoothness independently of each other.

Of all the known things about Fort McHenry, the most famous is Francis Scott Key and his writing of the "Star Spangled Banner" as a prisoner aboard an American truce ship. These lessons are taught in the classroom, but experiencing the lessons firsthand where it took place makes the learning of it more meaningful, said X.

It's unclear whether the problems here are traceable to the speaker X or to the author. The worst of these problems is the same one we saw above, a false compound subject. We're told this: The most famous of all the things known "is Francis Scott Key." FSK isn't a thing known. Presumably the most famous thing known is *the fact that* FSK wrote the "Star-Spangled Banner" while a prisoner aboard an American truce ship.

Yet even this is not unproblematic. Do most people know FSK's whereabouts? Probably the author's point is, the most famous fact is that FSK wrote the words to the SSB (NB: not the music: the article implies the whole song was written by FSK, which is factually incorrect) after viewing the battle over the Fort.

It's not clear what the "lesson" here is. The writer is confusing the sense of "Lesson 1, Lesson 2" in a textbook with the phrase "teach a lesson," which means show us a moral, make us sorry we did something.

"The learning of it [the lesson]" is off target as well as awkward. We use a gerund ("ing" form of verb used as a noun) to emphasize the progression of the action. We might say: "Learning this lesson was very painful." Here we're emphasizing the process of learning. The author here isn't emphasizing the process of learning; presumably it's the information itself that's "more meaningful." We don't say "The learning of it" the way we say "the meaning of it" (even here we'd say "its meaning"), at least not outside Ireland. [I've skipped here:] **X said the shaping of the Navy and its influence on building a strong nation was instrumental in not only winning the Battle of Baltimore, but making America what it is today.**

Another false compound subject. "X said" is followed by a clause ("that") with two subjects: "shaping" and "influence." Because there are two subjects, they require "*were* instrumental." But the author doesn't really mean that "shaping" is different from "influence." What, after all, does "shaping of the Navy" mean? He should say something like this: "X said the Navy was instrumental not only in winning the Battle of Baltimore, but also in building America into the strong nation it is today."

A lot of the seasonal employees said they really enjoyed being able to go into a greater level of detail about the fort's history with the midshipmen than is normally done with other visitors, said X.

We don't "go into a . . . level of detail." At most we can *attain* or *achieve* a greater level of detail. Probably the speaker is combining two phrases here, "go into greater detail" and "achieve a higher level of X." "Than is normally done" implies that what's preceded this is an action. Bill doesn't see the action. The author should summarize X as saying something like this: " lot of the seasonal employees said they really enjoyed being able to go into greater detail with the midshipmen than they usually can with other visitors, said X."

"It is really an honor to be able to do that. You can learn a lot in academics, you can learn a great deal in engineering, you can learn a great deal in athletics and stuff. But I think to have a deep sense of history is what really helps build character, that really makes future officers successful."

Why an honor? Because it's a rare opportunity to influence future officers? Perhaps, but Bill is just surmising here; too much fill-in is required on his part. "That'" presumably refers to going into greater detail, but Bill isn't sure.

It's confusing to Bill for the author to switch to the colloquial "You" in the phrase "you can learn" when the focus has been on what the *midshipmen* learn.

"Athletics and stuff"? What's "stuff"?

It's unclear what's going on in the last sentence. To have the sense of history builds character (an ongoing process)? Huh? You have the sense, and over time that produces the character? What's "that"? Having a deep sense of history? Having character?

What is it that makes future officers successful? Is it having character? Or having its building be helped by the study of history? Bill has more than a suspicion that a new sentence has been glued on to the old by the dreaded comma splice, so that the last part, beginning with "that" really means: " *That*, having character [still unclear what this means], makes officers successful."

But sir, you saw what I meant! Perhaps I did. But it took me way too much time, and it was way too painful. I only kept going because I had to. Nobody else will.

V
How to Read

Most of *Bill the Goat's Adult Refresher Guide to Writing* has been devoted, unsurprisingly, to writing. More specifically, writing for Bill. But reading also requires a few remarks. When you read, you see things from Bill's perspective

Sometimes we read things aimed, we know, at us. We're their Bill and can say immediately if the writing gets through to us or not. If it doesn't click, there's something wrong with it. Such writing fills small, well-defined holes that presuppose a lot of common knowledge. As a result they have very short life-spans, like insects that live a day or two, and tend not to be found outside the immediate area that produced them. Someone else's business memo or e-mail read by an outsider rarely makes much sense. It's food that, if not eaten immediately, goes bad.

Libraries, by contrast, are full of things meant to last. They're taken out of the time and place that produced them. For that matter, they're personal responses to questions nobody else but the author saw, so even if we could re-create the time and place that produced them we'd still be at a loss to say what the hole was they were filling. (Note the hyphen in "re-create" in this last sentence: it's there to prevent confusion with anything to do with a vacation or recess.) As a result, their Bills are frequently not clear. Let's say you check out a book. You don't know whether you're its Bill or not. You have to figure out who the book's Bill is. Can it be you? Figuring this out can be difficult, since answering this question means understanding the book.

Books, rather than office memos, are sometimes written for Bills defined by other qualities than sharing a single time and place, and presuppose less information accessible only to a small group of people. That's what makes them more transportable out of one context, and is the reason they stay around longer. There's also a scale within the category of "books." Yet another diet book will be aimed at a Bill that's specific in the world of books, even if its Bill is general when compared to the Bill of a memo. Novels aim at a more abstract Bill than cookbooks, and thus at a much more abstract Bill than a memo. More concrete books are easier to "place." It's the novels and the poetry that are difficult. Who is their audience? It's virtually impossible to answer this question from the other direction. Do you have to be black to like a novel with black characters? White to like a novel with white characters? Male to like a book about a man? (Or should this be: a woman?) The answer to these questions is, of course, no.

It's difficult to tell by looking at a person whether they're the Bill of a novel or not. Sometimes you can, at least to a limited degree. There's a gender edge in "chick lit" or "guy novels." And "gay fiction" has by and large not reached a non-gay audience. Still, there might be some crossovers in any of these groups, for whatever reason: whim, a friend's interest, or being caught at the beach with nothing else to read. In the case of "literary" fiction, which means precisely fiction not linked to easily definable groups in the world, the matching up of Bill with the book is complex and scatter-shoot.

1. *Strawberry preserves*

Let's focus one of the most abstract sorts of book: literary fiction. Poetry would do equally well as an example. These are what you're likely to get in a college course. Both are like preserved food rather than fresh.

Literary fiction isn't just a form of writing. It's a sort of content. The preservation that's taken place in a book transportable out of a particular context and that can survive in different times and places has determined its content. Only certain things preserve, and preserving alters the raw materials—more in some cases than others. We take for granted that strawberry preserves will be gooey, not made of whole berries; tomatoes become gushy in preservation rather than remaining globes. Things in cans rarely taste like fresh vegetables. The conventions of literary fiction are transformations of content that allow preservation outside the specific context of writing. What it considers is going to be what we think of as big issues, not the trivia of daily intercourse, otherwise there's no point to preserving it. We have enough of our own trivia.

Most people would say that the defining quality of fiction is that it isn't true: it's made up. But much of what's in a novel *is* true: the sky is up, people in the West eat with knives and forks, and most people have two legs. Conversely, a novel can simply be wrong: people in Victorian England didn't wear mini-skirts and the automobile hadn't yet been invented. If we read a novel with these errors, we'd call them this—unless they were so consistently followed out and developed that the result was a fantasy, or a satire—but we'd have to see this too. If a novel called the mid-to-late nineteenth-century queen of England "Queen Arabella" with no visible reason, we'd object. What happened to Queen Victoria? we'd say. And historical fiction that tells us what real people thought or felt is always grating. We think: how does the author know?

Novels have developed in the way they did because a book about a Mary Reilly, a kitchen maid in Bath in the 1880s, that tells us what she thought and felt, poses none of the problems of a novel about Queen Victoria that supplies her inner feelings. A novel about Mary Reilly is like somebody telling us stories about what's beyond the mountains where no one has ever gone. In neither case do we know for sure; we express this by saying the story is plausible: it jibes with what we do know. Both stories in what I call the gray area of our knowledge.

The response will be: No, stories about beyond the mountains are different than stories about Mary Reilly because someone *could* go beyond the mountains and show the stories to be correct or incorrect. We can't find out about Mary Reilly; she's only made up. But that's going from the wrong direction, assuming that the "made up" part makes her different. Besides, we *can* learn so much about the world that is true in a novel (Bath is true, 1880s is true, hansom cabs is true) that we can say for sure whether a kitchen maid named Mary Reilly in this part of town is right or wrong. It's just that we don't, because she's plausible now with respect to what we know (as a novel about Queen Victoria might not be); all more information would do would be to push forward the frontier of knowledge so that plausible recedes just that amount. More facts might well make a novel about Mary Reilly impossible. But do we know about all, say, cats alive then? If we knew everything about people, novels would be about cats, until we learned about every individual cat.

A novel about proper-name people, such as Queen Victoria, puts front and center things we're conscious of having learned. For this reason, we're very conscious when the author suddenly talks about things that nobody can ever know, the equivalent of information about heaven (you have to die to get there), in the midst of facts whose truth we're able to decide upon. It's the shift that bothers us, not the fact that we don't know. The most important question is thus not, Is this real or made up? It's, instead: When do we not care whether something is made up or not? We don't care if stories about Mary Reilly are made up or not: perhaps we like the uncertainty of being situated in the gray area. Similarly we may not care if stories about the world beyond the mountains, even if told by someone who didn't go there (perhaps that someone has other ways of knowing?), are true or false. That just isn't a question we're interested in asking.

The gray area is a real place, just as "I don't know" is frequently the (true) answer to questions. The gray area also exists with respect to beliefs as well as knowledge. Many things we'd say we believe, only we've never even articulated it to the extent of saying that. Do I believe that the floor will support me when I step on it? Do I believe I can swim through the water? That water is wet? Sure, why not? Give me a reason for not believing these things, we'd say. But in any individual case the floor can, of course, fall through; I can fail to swim through the water; and the water might in some technical sense I can't currently articulate not be (or feel?) wet. I don't so much believe these things as see no reason to question them.

Leaving things in the gray area is antithetical to people who haven't understood that the gray area is all around us. Nobody has pointed out to them all the things they simply don't ask about in the world outside fiction that are also in the gray area, so they're in the habit of thinking this quality is one of fiction alone, rather than being true of much of the world. We have to have a reason to ask questions; usually we lack this.

2. New ways of seeing

Sometimes people say: "A classic is a work you can always see in a new way."

This is wrong. Though I re-read *Madame Bovary* almost every year to teach it, I don't see a different work each time. At best I'm reminded of things I've forgotten. A small handful of times I've tried works at different times of my life and found a work either that I suddenly understood the second time, or that I found I'd grown out of. But what this measures is the change in me, not in the work.

I think what people really mean when they say this is that there is a wide range of variation between people, not between one reading and the next: two people in, say, the same class find two different aspects interesting. But why should this be surprising? The work we read in a class is almost inevitably going to be far from home, historically and culturally speaking. And the fact that two people sit next to each other in the class in the same here and now doesn't mean they are at all alike as people.

3. Gizmos

Literary fiction pays a price for its preservability. Namely, that it's a bit alien. We come upon it there, usually sitting on a shelf. We have to decide whether it's worth the effort to take it away, or whether we should merely put it back and continue on. Except in the situation of a professor requiring it for us to pass a course and get a degree, our lives will continue (for all we know) just fine without it. Yet if we do take it with us we may find our lives changed utterly.

There are many books we don't connect with at all. That's what browsing in a bookstore tells us. A few pages is enough in many cases. In the case of a standard work read in a class, the assumption is that lots of people have gotten something from this, so perhaps we should plough on for a while longer, and not be discouraged by failing to find our twin—same age, race, religion, and nationality and so, of course, fascinating—on the first page. We have to choose to include literature in our lives: it doesn't press itself on us. Only writing at the other end of the spectrum does that, the clear office memo or response e-mail. A novel is like a gizmo that catches our eye in the corner of an antique shop. The idle browser picks it up, wonders for a minute what it might be, and puts it back. The curious person takes it home and tries to figure it out. That means, figure out its Bill.

Asking, Who is the author's Bill? does not mean, what group of people was this intended for? It asks, what is being taken for granted and what new information is being given? What group does this define? Nor does it assert that people actually understood it this way, or that the Bill the work postulates existed in historical fact.

As the New Critics and their progeny pointed out, there's no way to know the author's intention because the author is probably dead and has probably left no document behind that announce "My intentions in writing work X were A, B, and C." Even if the author had left such a document, or were alive to answer this question, who says that this answer would be the truth? Authors are fallible and forget their intentions, or don't always answer questions truthfully. Besides, what do intentions matter when you have the text? My students are full of all sorts of intentions that never make it to Bill.

Many adult readers know that the text has to mean something other than merely the facts it offers. But they have no idea how to access meaning. My students think they have no alternative but throwing themselves on the mercy of outside authority. Only a priestly figure, like the professor, can explain what they call the "deep meaning" of a text. So they're content to fill the class time saying a little of this and a little of that with the expectation that a few minutes before the end of class, I will pull the rabbit out of the hat and show them the "deep" meaning they can never hope to access on their own.

I don't pull rabbits out of hats. Besides, I dislike the metaphor of depth with literary texts. It's all on the surface, as I insist to my disbelieving students. They just have to look at the surface more carefully than they do. They need to put themselves in Bill's position.

Sometimes, to be sure, there's something I know that the students can't learn by reading carefully, as for example what the author does with this theme in other works. Or how other works of the time do things. Or what a particular word means. Sometimes it makes sense to acknowledge problems with difficult lines in, say, Shakespeare or the English Romantics. So there may be a legitimate reason to speed things up by giving an answer, just for the sake of being efficient.

But an adult reader should be able to figure out most everything in a text that can be figured, barring such footnotable things as archaic words and strange references. My students, and most readers, lounge by the side of the road, waiting for a ride, when they could get to their destination just fine on foot. It's actually not as far away as they think. They broad-jump the text and then sit back, waiting for the professor to give them the deep meaning.

Broad-jumping a text never leads to understanding it. Really reading a text is a completely different sensation. It's like wading through hip-high mud. You're supposed to feel every step.

4. Two kinds of not understanding

Readers who assume that texts are not something they can themselves have any relationship to—who assume that they simply bat a ball back and forth for 49 minutes while in the 50th minute the professor/priest pulls the rabbit from a hat and they go home—conclude from the fact that it feels the same to not understand a text that nobody can understand as it does to not understand a piece of nonsense that in fact, they are identical. *I've left this sentence as I first wrote it as an example of overdriving my headlights and of several other problems. I can keep all these ideas in the same breath because I know where it's going. But it's all too much for Bill. So, revised, laying out the cards one, two, three, and fixing the other mistakes:*

Second (better) try: My students frequently assume they can watch the magician [the metaphor was what we call "mixed," combining tennis with a magic show] idly for 49 of the class's 50 minutes [Bill probably doesn't know that classes at the Naval Academy are 50 minutes, so I have to tell him] until, in the 50th minute, the professor/magician pulls the rabbit from the hat and they can go. They do this because they assume that texts are not something they can have any relationship to ["they themselves" is redundant]. Thus they insist that there is no intrinsic difference between a bad text, that can never be figured out, and a good one, which can be figured out with time. If you're not actively involved in trying to figure out a text, the state of not (yet) understanding a good text is identical to the state of not understanding a bad one (where there's nothing to understand). They can't see a reason for distinguishing between a good work and a bad one, because they're in the same state with respect to both kinds.

A good text is good because it reveals more the more you look. It returns the investment; it gives its Bill a good run. A bad text constantly kicks its Bill in the shins, and ends up alienating him utterly. He was ready to run before, but now he's not.

For readers waiting for the rabbit to be pulled from the hat, "yet to be figured out" feels the same as "can't be figured out." Thus when they're writers, they're contented with being unclear to Bill. They don't sense the difference between merely being off the path, on one hand, and, on the other, being off the path but relating to it in an interesting way.

If they don't know how to go about answering their own questions, I worry, how will they grow into fully mature reader-adults? There won't always be someone around to give them answers. At some point they're on their own. If they don't know how to ask the questions, they'll be limited to those texts where they're the most evident Bill—memos, for example, or self-help books for their particular problems. They'll never have the sense of limitless possibility we get opening a book that wasn't meant just for us, or the sense of humility before the world it produces.

5. Guidance

One unread work is identical to another, so long as both remain unread. It's equally true that there are far more works in the world than any mortal can read. Good works give you a return on your investment and bad works don't. So you have to make intelligent choices about where to invest your time. Most people can do with some guidance. Perhaps we pick our books by remembering the authors we read in college, by reading the book reviews, or by following who wins the prizes. All this is common sense, just the way you scan the movie listings to eliminate the total junk—or to aim for it, if that's the mood you're in. But there's no guarantee you'll always get something from every one of the books on this short list, or that by using the usual channels you'll find the one book that might change your life. Perhaps the one book for you is totally unknown, or comes to your attention through a personal recommendation.

So take chances. Pick up books on a whim. Browse in bookstores. Listen to people you trust and try out their recommendation. Your highest single return may be on something that initially didn't seem so promising. If you turn out not to like it, you can always stop reading.

6. Notice things

Here are the steps to figuring out a work's Bill if you don't know whether or not that Bill is you.

Notice things. The first step in figuring out who the Bill is in work of literature is, What does the work presuppose its Bill knows? What's new information for him? What Bill presupposes defines the "inside" for the work: things it merely refers to, without explaining. Every work has an "outside" as well: the things it has to tell the reader. Typically in fiction the outside will focus on the particular fictional characters, made fictional by the fact that this text is where we come for information about them. Many facts about their world will be part of the shared background that defines inside, the solid land with the hole.

Justify that assertion. If you say that Character X is Adjective Y (lazy, sullen, happy, ambitious), you have to be able to provide justification to what you say. "Here she says A, or does B; this is a repeated pattern; there is little or no sign of behavior that is the opposite of Adjective Y)." Things don't always have to be clear: maybe what you say is precisely that we see conflicting behavior on the part of the character. Or that we can't figure out what the character is like.

Think structurally. If there is no visible pattern of any sort in the new, outside, information that's given Bill, the work has no point. (See the John Cage exception considered above: the point is the lack of pattern. But that too is a pattern, and has to be made explicit. There's a difference between a work about the lack of pattern and a work without a pattern.) Articulate that pattern. It can be found in the relationship between the characters, or in the relation between the state of events at the beginning of the work and the end.

7. The blind man

Frequently a short story begins with a static situation that the events of the story bring to a head or alter. Be able to articulate what the beginning situation is, and why it changes as a result of these events. In D.H. Lawrence's short story "The Blind Man," for example, the story clearly changes from a state at the beginning to another state at the end. An intellectual woman, married to a less cerebral but loving man who's been blinded in World War I, senses him going downhill emotionally. She's increasingly unable to cope with his depression, which she knows is somehow related to their isolation and to his blindness.

The situation is unstable. The wife is pregnant, and she fears the baby will isolate her to an even greater degree from her husband, and him from her. If the subsequent events of the story do not somehow relate to this situation, that's going to be a flaw of the story. We'd say it doesn't make sense. What we'd mean is, there's no visible pattern, or the pattern is shaky, or full of contradictory evidence.

My students go to many movies that, in this sense, are based on shaky structures. What the (say) heroine does simply doesn't make sense. What does she see in this man whom we're asked to believe is the love of her life? Why wouldn't she have left him long before? Why are we asked to believe X, Y, and Z when they're clearly improbable in this situation? For most people, going to the movies is a time when you let your mind go blank. So it's only critics who are likely to point out these problems. Still, movies that show weakness on repeated viewings aren't good candidates for immortality.

Anthologized short stories, because they have survived, tend to be the stories that lack such mistakes. Turned around positively, this means they reward concentration rather than disappoint it. They justify the hope we have when we begin a new work. My students don't understand what I mean when I try to express this sensation. They've never felt the letdown of trying to make a written work make sense and being disappointed because the only literary fiction they read was in an English class. It was chosen for them; they didn't have to read all the also-rans to decide on this one.

As a result they think that authors are merely celebrities: they're famous for being famous, so you read their stories. Sometimes I think I ought to mix mediocre or bad stories on my syllabus with the good ones, so students can get a sense of what it means to try and figure out a story and be stymied because the story doesn't have a coherent enough pattern, or gives conflicting information, or ends in a banal point, or doesn't have any point. That way they'd see the difference between good and bad.

In Lawrence's short story, the particular events are in fact related to this initial situation. An estranged cousin of the wife's writes to ask if he may come to visit. The indication that something is about to change is that the husband, who didn't get along with the quick-witted but somehow creepy cousin, is suddenly willing (eager?) to have him come.

Would we say that the husband is merely willing to have the cousin come now? Or that, going further, he's actually eager? Lawrence doesn't give us enough information to decide this one. It's possible that the husband himself doesn't know. Yet if we can't decide whether the husband is willing or eager, all this means is that there's not enough evidence to say. So that's what we say: we say what's given and what's not. Similarly, if the actions of a character remain ambiguous after consideration, they remain ambiguous. We don't have to make them be something clearer that they're not. Students typically laugh with relief when I tell them this. I'm trying to show them how to notice things. If they don't find them after looking, that itself is what they've noticed.

8. Touch

The most basic thing to notice in "The Blind Man" is that the two men get along very badly indeed. That's what we would have expected from the fact that Lawrence characterizes them in such opposing terms. (I tell the students: list what you know about each character.) The husband is slow, almost bestial, constantly compared to the cows he tends (the students have to identify the language in which this occurs) or to trees, rooted in the Earth. And he's blind, related in standard language to a deficiency of intellect ("you don't *see* my point"). The husband is stereotypically male, unable to articulate but strong, good for heavy work. He's impregnated his wife, so he's male in that sense too.

The cousin, in almost cartoon-like contrast, is completely aphysical, a small man, but quick-witted. We're told he pushes away women who become too close, and there's no indication he gets along any better with men. In fact, he seems himself to be neither male nor female (or perhaps: neither masculine nor feminine). The word Lawrence uses to describe him is "neuter." Not being able to say precisely what this means is precisely what you say.

When this situation changes abruptly, as it does toward the end of the story, we're clearly supposed to notice it—because in a sense we're waiting for it. Otherwise the story would be too banal. The scene occurs near the end where the cousin comes out to the husband's home turf, the stables, in the dark. The dark is scary to a seeing man, but comforting to a blind man. The husband asks the cousin first what his scar looks like: is it awful? He then asks the cousin to touch his eye sockets. We know this is going to pose problems given the cousin's morbid fear of any sort of physical intimacy. (Lawrence has spelled this out for us.)

"Why can't he ask this of his wife?" I ask the students. "Why do we need the cousin in the story at all?" The more general version of this question for all fiction is: Why have things been set up the way they're set up? In bad stories, novels, or movies, we frequently can't answer this question. No beaten path is established, so we can't articulate anything as being off of it.

The students think a bit, and then realize that the wife would by definition say her husband looked fine. To get an objective answer to his question, the husband needs to talk to another man—not to another woman, given the formulaic nature of verbal exchange between men and women at the time, and certainly not his wife, who will not be objective. If a man tells him his scar is awful, that at least is something concrete that he can begin to accept with time. Having the other man touch the wound and live would be further objectification. It wouldn't seem awful.

In Lawrence's story, the husband is exhilarated at having the other man touch him—the cousin is too cowed to refuse—and comes in the house glowing, to announce to the wife that he's found a friend. That's not the case, as Lawrence makes clear. He tells us the cousin is "like a mollusk whose shell has been broken." The wife, who sees her cousin's face and knows him well, can tell too that her husband is mistaken. She may realize simultaneously that his inevitable disappointment will send him even deeper into his spiral of depression.

Adding up what we've figured out, we can say this is a story about a man who wanted something from another man, and didn't get it, perhaps because the other man fate threw his way was abnormally unsuited to fill that role. It's a story about a last chance that failed, a story with an unhappy ending.

9. Mickey's three fingers

It's not surprising that students delight in offering "naughty" explanations of the data, given their affection for rabbits pulled out of hats. They can't be proven wrong, but I get them to point out that there's no reason to accept these over other explanations either. Or they offer explanations that work with two data points in the work but do not explain conflicting data that point in other directions.

I wish I had a dollar for every time a student has said, "Sir, it's just a poem/story/novel. You can say anything you want about it." Not only students, but many adult readers are ready to throw up their hands at literature and say, "You can say anything." They lack confidence in their own powers to think the problem out. It's easier to give up right away.

My first job is to prove to them that you can't, in fact, say "anything" about literature.

I ask, "Is it about why Mickey has three fingers on each hand?" No, they finally say. It's not about Mickey's three fingers.

"Why not?" I demand. "I say it is. If literature is about anything you say it's about, I say it's about Mickey's three fingers. Convince me it isn't." Now the shoe is on the other foot. They shift uncomfortably in their seats.

Then they say: "Because there's no reason to say this."

Explanations for things in the world as well as in literature are rarely clearly correct or clearly incorrect, especially in the early stages of arriving at them. Instead, we have to justify them as being more or less useful explanations of the data. We need to get as much data as we can and not close any out, and we need explanations that cover the largest percentage of these data. The process is arduous with literature, but it's arduous with the world too. Why do people give up immediately with literature but not with the rest of the world? Can it be that they're not used to anything printed at any location on the spectrum other than that of the office memo?

10. *The Martians came*

If we go out of our way to propose such explanations for life that can neither be proven nor disproven, we can be just as inventive. Most people would say, I'm a professor teaching a class at the U.S. Naval Academy. Yet, based on the data available to the students, it's equally possible I'm an agent of X sent to gather information, or a cunningly designed machine, or that what I take to be midshipmen are in fact agents of Y. But why would I say any of these? Sure they're possible, but they're not probable, and I have no evidence that they're so.

Hollywood delights in such "looks normal but isn't" situations; one of the more striking movies of this sort is the original *Manchurian Candidate* of John Frankenheimer. The young man around whom the movie turns seemed to be a war hero but was in fact a brainwashed tool of his fiendish mother. Another, similar movie, *No Way Out*, showed what seemed to be a nice American boy, a LCDR in the U.S. Navy, who in fact was a Soviet spy.

In the case of *The Manchurian Candidate*, the antagonist figured things out: there was evidence to suggest that things were not as they had seemed. There were slip-ups by the bad guys that led him to the truth: all the people who had been with the purported war hero used exactly the same words to describe his "heroic" exploits; the young man himself had recurring nightmares that were about what turned out to be the real events (the situation of brainwashing).

But it's possible things could have been so smooth there were no slip-ups and we could still, with no evidence whatever, assert these goofy explanations for things. I call this "the Martians came last night." "Really? Where are the traces of their coming?" "They were so smart they made them all disappear."

11. Descartes' razor

Descartes too worried about similar questions: could what he took to be a man walking outside his window in fact be a machine? Descartes decided that probably the usual explanations were true (it's a man down there, not a machine) because God existed and wasn't a trickster.

Other people invoke "Occam's razor": the principle that you should minimize your explanation unless you're forced to expand it. It's possible this isn't a dandelion in my front yard but a sophisticated listening device planted by the KGB. However if I have no evidence that this is so, I shouldn't go around saying it is. But there's no good reason ever given for Occam's razor: it presupposes that simplicity has some intrinsic virtue that complexity lacks.

The best reason I know for not multiplying possible but unjustified explanations of the world is that they're too easy to produce, and because they run counter to the things we take for granted (dandelions are dandelions) they require a lot of mental energy for others to process. We can give a million possible but unjustified explanations for things: I'm (you're) an agent of the KGB, of Osama bin Laden, of X, of Y... This blade of grass isn't what it seems, nor the next one, nor the next one... It's possible I'm a Martian, even if I believe I'm not (the secret here is implanted memory, as in the movie *Blade Runner*). Everything that seems normal can be postulated not to be normal, so long as we don't ask for justification.

12. Forks

We can say with some degree of certainty that "The Blind Man" is not about why Mickey has three fingers on each hand, nor (my other favorite example) about looking both ways when you cross the street. So that's already something we know. So what is it about? Perhaps, I suggest, it's about male relationships? Usually the midshipmen accept that there's evidence pointing in this direction. Can it also be about the power of touch? We have justification for that too.

This seems to them like a fork in the road: we have to choose one or the other. Students frequently confuse such forks in the road with complete lack of path. If we ever get to a point where I say, "I can accept either X or Y," a certain number of them always sit back vindicated. "See?" says their body language, if not their mouths. "I told you you can say anything you want."

But working up to the point where we hit a fork doesn't mean all the path is the fork. There are many questions we can answer about literature with a high degree of certainty. How old is the main character? Ballpark figure? What adjectives do we accept with respect to him/her? Why? What does A do when B does X? Can we say why?

In life outside of literature, we can answer a slew of smaller questions with great certainty. How old am I? Am I typing this on a computer? Is this a picture of my family on the side of the desk? What time is it?

But good luck with questions like, Is human life more joy or more sorrow? Or: What makes a certain configuration of atoms "alive"? (We can't say: brain waves, thought, feelings etc—those are effects or products of being alive.) My personal favorite among the unanswerable questions is this one: Do we learn more as we age? Or do we just learn different things? The fact that some questions are unanswerable doesn't mean they all are.

14. Reading Shakespeare

Othello in the tragedy named after him is a character who appeals to many students at the Naval Academy, once we help them see what's going on in the play. He's a man's man, someone who has lived the military life since an early age. He says he's a plain-spoken man who doesn't use complex words, and who knows only about war and the military. Here's how he describes himself:

> **Rude am I in my speech,**
> **And little blessed with the soft phrase of peace.**
> **For since these arms of mine had seven years pith**
> **Till now some nine moons wasted, they have used**
> **Their dearest action in the tented field,**
> **And little of this great world can I speak**
> **More than pertains to fears of broils and battles;**
> **And therefore little shall I grace my cause**
> **In speaking for myself.** (I, iii., l. 81 ff.)

From the time he was seven until nine months ago, he's lived in the tented field, involved in war. Because of his new job, he suddenly finds himself in a world he doesn't understand: a city world, a world of primping men (Desdemona has turned down "curled darlings" as suitors) and people with the time to develop their turns of phrase. He's fallen hard for a woman, and things moved so quickly she's eloped with him. As we might expect, things have started going wrong immediately. Othello been hauled—in the middle of his wedding night, no less—before the ruling council of Venice, for whom he works as what we would call a mercenary admiral (that's the way they did it in Venice at the time), to answer the charges of his friend Brabantio that's he's enchanted Brabantio's daughter Desdemona, now Othello's wife. [You should see why I've repeated all these proper nouns here: if I'd just said "he" we wouldn't be able to follow.] This is the only reason Brabantio can think that Desdemona should have run off with Othello and married him. Brabantio likes Othello as a buddy, it seems, but not as a son-in-law.

Othello is very conscious of coming up short by the standards of the Venetians; it's only with other men in the "tented field" that he feels secure. He can't talk as well as the city boys, because he doesn't know how to act in "chambers" rather than in the field. Easily convinced by Iago that Desdemona is unfaithful to him, he quickly lists his shortcomings: it seems to him logical that he's been left for someone of Desdemona's own skin color, who's younger, more refined, and better looking—one Michael Cassio, to whom (as it turns out) Desdemona is quite indifferent.

**Haply for I am black
And have not those soft parts of conversation
That chamberers have, or for that I am declined
Into the vale of years—yet that's not much—
She's gone.** (III,iii. 265 ff)

It's clear Othello is somewhat darker-skinned than the Venetians, but we don't know how much. Moors—the sub-title of the play is "The Moor of Venice"—are Northern Africans, part of what is sometimes called "White Africa." Othello, however, may be black as he's sometimes called "the thick-lips" and his bosom is described as "sooty." We don't know if these are relative adjectives, as someone who is a slight bit darker than white could be called "black," or even if they're purposely exaggerated, as they only occur in moments when the speaker is angry with Othello.

Any man is likely to be upset at the thought of his wife having found another sexual partner. But Othello's agony, fueled by his sense of being in foreign territory not only literally but metaphorically, seems extreme, and drives him to truly horrific comparisons. Here he compares himself, unfavorably, to an imprisoned, starving toad.

> **O curse of marriage**
> **That we can call these delicate creatures ours,**
> **And not their appetites! I had rather be a toad**
> **And live upon the vapor of a dungeon**
> **Than keep a corner in the thing I love**
> **For others' uses.**

Because he's a warrior, Othello is tough and can deal with any direct affliction; what he can't deal with is uncertainty coupled with the horror of having been betrayed after straying from the world in which he was comfortable, the world of battle and men. "Villain," he enjoins Iago in what initially seems a strange command, "Be sure thou prove my love a whore!" (III, iii., 365). Othello exhibits the distinctly male, perhaps peculiarly military need to have absolute trust in another person: that's what he's needed with subordinates, after all. Lack of knowledge is lack of control: "**I swear 'tis better to be much abused/ Than to know but a little**" (III, iii, l. 334). Uncertainty is worse than certainty of a much worse thing.

> **I had been happy if the general camp,**
> **Pioners [soldiers/grunts] and all, had tasted her sweet body,**
> **So I had nothing known. O now, forever**
> **Farewell the tranquil mind! Farewell content!**
> **Farewell the plumed troops, and the big wars**
> **That make ambition virtue! O, farewell!**
> **Farewell the neighing steed and the shrill trump,**
> **The spirit-stirring drum, th' ear-piercing fife,**
> **The royal banner, and all quality,**
> **Pride, pomp, and circumstance of glorious war!** (III, iii, 342 ff).

Othello's his not knowing what's going on with his wife means the end of his military career: he's lost his faith in the possibility of absolute knowledge even of men in the military. Still, at least he gets to keep his absolute trust in one person. It's the irony of the play that that one person is Iago. The other men of the "tented field" are gone; at least in the confines of the play everything seems reduced to the individuals now, uncharacteristically, taking center stage in Othello's mind. It's the world of individuals where Othello feels out of his element. Thus the play is about what happens when someone who sees people as means to an end, a military commander, has to confront them as individuals: from puppet master, Othello becomes the puppet. Perhaps Shakespeare's point is that turn about is fair play: those who use individuals as means to an end will themselves be used in the same fashion.

Iago offers Othello the choice between male bonding with his subordinate, and the bond he's not sure of, with Desdemona. Desdemona doesn't stand a chance. Iago's logic is very convincing because it makes sense: why would Desdemona be in love with an older, dark-skinned foreigner? Chances are wildly against it, as Othello admits. But the ironic joke of the play is that Desdemona is in fact in love with Othello, despite the improbability of her being so.

The image of the toad returns when Othello is hurting the most. He reiterates that he's able to take any degree of physical punishment. That after all is what the life of the soldier entails. What he can't stand is knowing he went against character by giving into his tender feelings (feelings he may not even have known he had) and paying so dearly for doing so: it's as if he's furious with himself for having been so dumb. (The "gotcha" of the play is that though Desdemona's being in love with Othello was a long shot, it's one that came through for Othello: she is in love with him. The problem isn't where logic and Othello's good sense would suggest it would be, in Desdemona's feelings for Othello, but in Iago, where it doesn't occur to Othello it could possibly be.)

Here's what he says when he's at his most miserable:

> **Had it pleased heaven**
> **To try me with affliction, had they rained**
> **All kinds of sores and shames on my bare head,**
> **Steeped me in poverty to the very lips,**
> **Given to captivity me and my utmost hopes,**
> **I should have found in some place of my soul**
> **A drop of patience. But alas, to make me**
> **The fixed figure for the time of scorn**
> **To point his slow and moving finger at.**
> **Yet could I bear that too, well, very well.**

> **But there where I have garnered up my heart,**
> **Where either I must live or bear no life,**
> **The fountain from the which my current runs**
> **Or else dries up—to be discarded thence,**
> **Or keep it as a cistern for foul toads**
> **To knot and gender in—** (IV, ii, 46 ff.)

The thought of being a figure of scorn is horrible enough; he's a man whose honor is his identity. (The image is of scorn itself pointing a finger at him.) Yet worse than that is having found, and given in to his tender feelings (located, then as now, at least in common speech in the heart), and being betrayed. For Othello it's much worse to have loved and lost than never to have loved at all, because he was a functional man's man when he hadn't loved, and now that he has loved and been (so he thinks) been betrayed, he's ruined.

How oddly his mind runs, in this most horrific of images: the place where his heart was turned to an empty well-like container, the heart banished, the empty space not holding any liquid but dark and dampness, in the corners of which toads "knot and gender." His heart is a damp dark emptiness containing only copulating toads. It seems he wants to crawl out of his own skin; literature contains few passages that so clearly give us this sense of self-loathing and self-fury. He's done it to himself—or so he thinks. He does do it to himself, but, ironically, not in the way he imagines: the whole play is an essay on the fact that the universe really doesn't seem to be amenable to logic or understanding.

Othello is Shakespeare's portrait of a man who is confident with men in a world where he's comfortable, yet is riddled with insecurities when faced with the less predictable side of life: relationships with the opposite sex, or domestic as opposed to military life. It's a meditation on the inability of the individual to nail down the world: the more you get it nailed down in one sector, *Othello* reminds us, the less able you are to deal with the slipping uncertainties of the rest of the world. The military life gives us the illusion of a certainty we have no right to have.

What do I tell Bill?

Bill the Goat's Adult Refresher Guide to Writing has tried to show you how to deal with the uncertainties of writing: is it X or Y? Do I say it this way or that way? There's no fixed answer: instead you have to ask, what do I want to tell Bill? And that will help you find the answer.

Answers are specific to your own situation, your own Bill. What's eternal is the process of looking for them.

There is no list of writing "how-tos" complete enough to cover all the situations that you come across, or that will ever be. Each person reacts to the world s/he finds, which means, takes what is and either reiterates it or builds on it. You do this by using in rapid-fire succession and in no particular order all of the things you know about communicating in language with another person, and about writing.

Writing is not a skill separable from what you have to say on the page, it's how you say what you say on the page. It can be more effective or less effective. To make it more effective, you need to write for Bill. And get some sleep.

Index

Addams, Charles, 99
adjectives, co-ordinate, 74
adjectives, non-coordinate, 74
appositive, restrictive, 75
appositive, non- restrictive, 75
Asperger's Syndrome, 52
Baby Bill, 42
ballparking, 37
Blade Runner, 136
Bogart, Humphrey
   Dark Passage, 91
Brigade of Midshipmen, 9
Cage, John, 131
   4'2", 14
clause, non-restrictive, 75
clause, restrictive, 75
clause, subordinate, 67
clichés, 36
Clinton, Bill, 52
clusters (punctuation), 71
colon, 79
comma splice, 78
commas, 71
conjunctions, co-ordinating, 81
conjunctions, subordinating, 81
Dark Passage
   Bogart, Humphrey, 91
Derrida, Jacques, 33
Descartes, René, 136
descriptive grammar, 48
Detroit News, The, 38

Dickinson, Emily, 50
diction, 100
discourse, indirect, 87
Elements of Style, The
   Strunk and White, 8
e-mail, 1
Faulkner, William, 15
five-paragraph essay, 10
Flaubert, Gustave
   Madame Bovary, 76
Fleming, Bruce
   Twilley, 61
foregrounding meanings, 93
Foucault, Michel, 33
Frankenheimer, John
   Manchurian Candidate, The, 135
Gore, Al, 52
grammar "gotcha", 49
Houdini, Harry, 19
hyphen, 79
"if" clause, 89
infinitive, split, 53
inspection, 20
Instant Message, 1
Keats, John
   "Ode on a Grecian Urn", 76
Kennedy, Jacqueline, 126
Language Instinct, The
   Pinker, Stephen, 52
langue/parole
   Saussure, Ferdinand de, 93
Lawrence, D. H.
   "The Blind Man", 131

lists (commas), 73
Manchurian Candidate, The
    Frankenheimer, John, 135
memorandum, 9
metaphors, 98
Michelangelo, 21
Mickey Mouse, 134
New Critics, 33, 128
New Yorker, The, 99
No Way Out, 135
Occam's razor, 136
openers, 58
Othello
    Shakespeare, William, 137
paragraphs, 62
parallelism, 83
pattern completion, 68
Pinker, Stephen
    Language Instinct, The, 52
predicate, compound, 67
prescriptive grammar, 48
Proust, Marcel
    Remembrance of Things Past, 61
punctuation, 69
reference, pronoun, 35, 82
Remembrance of Things Past
    Proust, Marcel, 61
revision, 44
Saussure, Ferdinand de
    langue/parole, 93
semi-colon, 78
sentence, compound, 67

sentences, 64
Shakespeare, William, 22
    Hamlet, 96
    Othello, 137
    Sonnet 55, 72, 95
Shelley, Percy, 98
Strunk and White
    Elements of Style, The, 8, 10, 13
"Superman," 83
"that"/"which", 77
"The Blind Man"
    Lawrence, D. H., 131
topic, 54
topic sentence, 58
Tractatus logico-philosophicus
    Wittgenstein, Ludwig, 63
Twilley
    Fleming, Bruce, 61
U.S. Naval Academy, 2, 9, 23, 45, 51, 63
verb tense, 86
Victoria, Queen, 125
voice, passive, 91
Washington Post, The, 38
which/that, 77
Wittgenstein, Ludwig
    Tractatus logico-philosophicus, 63
Wodehouse, P.G., 73
word usage, 92

About the Author

Bruce Fleming won an O. Henry Award for his first published story, "The Autobiography of Gertrude Stein" (1991) and in 2005, the Antioch Review Award for Distinguished Prose, a career award. His experimental novel *Twilley* (1997) was compared by critics to works by Henry James, T.S. Eliot, Proust, Thoreau, and David Lynch. He has published a book of dance essays, *Sex, Art and Audience* (2000), many scholarly and theoretical books, and articles and essays in literary quarterlies and publications such as the *Village Voice*, *The Washington Post*, and *The Nation*. His most recent books include *Life, Death and Literature at the U.S. Naval Academy* (2005), *Why Liberals and Conservatives Clash* (2006) and *The New Tractatus* (2007). He is an English professor at the U.S. Naval Academy, Annapolis, where he has taught literature and writing for more than twenty years.

www.ingramcontent.com/pod-product-compliance
Lightning Source LLC
Chambersburg PA
CBHW021129300426
44113CB00006B/347